AMERICAN
MUSIC
IS

AMERICAN
MUSIC
IS

Nat Hentoff

Da Capo Press
A Member of the Perseus Books Group

Set in 11-point Trump Mediaeval by The Perseus Books Group

Cataloging-in-Publication data for this book is available from the Library of Congress.

First Da Capo Press edition 2004
ISBN 0-306-81351-3

Published by Da Capo Press
A Member of the Perseus Books Group
http://www.dacapopress.com

Da Capo Press books are available at special discounts for bulk purchases in the U.S. by corporations, institutions, and other organizations. For more information, please contact the Special Markets Department at the Perseus Books Group, 11 Cambridge Center, Cambridge, MA 02142, or call (800) 255-1514 or (617) 252-5298, or e-mail special.markets@perseusbooks.com.

1 2 3 4 5 6 7 8 9   08 07 06 05 04

"Music is your own experience, your thoughts, your wisdom. If you don't live it, it won't come out of your horn. They teach you there's a boundary line to music. But man, there's no boundary line to art."

— CHARLIE PARKER

For my swinging grandchildren:
Elliana, Keaton, Kellin, Hugo, and Story.

Contents

Contents

Contents

Contents

Contents

ACKNOWLEDGMENTS

This book would not have been possible were it not for the encouragement, at the *Wall Street Journal*, of Eric Gibson, and his predecessor, Ray Sokolov, editors of the Leisure & Arts page. And, at *JazzTimes*, publisher Lee Mergner. Not many editors these days would suffer a writer who still uses a typewriter (what might be called acoustic journalism).

At Da Capo, I am grateful to Dan O'Neil and, of course, to publisher John Radziewicz who, like the music in this book, is uncategorizable.

I am also indebted to the encouragement and persistence of my literary agent, Richard Morris, who kept on keeping on. He was my rhythm section. So was Carmel Huestis of Perseus Books Group.

As always, I am in debt to the musicians, so generous of time and patience in the interviews for *American Music Is!* Merle Haggard once told me that when everything else gets him down, it's music that keeps him going. I told him these life sounds keep me going too. And I am privileged to have gotten to know, in and out of their music, so many of these originals who keep ringing the liberty bell.

INTRODUCTION

I never told him, but Sidney Bechet—who came out of New Orleans like a typhoon—was responsible for my dropping out of Harvard Graduate School when I was 20. One Sunday night, in Widener Library, I was researching a paper on James Fenimore Cooper and the Indians, but kept being distracted by an imperious call. I knew that Bechet, at that moment, was lifting his long, thrusting soprano saxophone to hurl his musicians and the listeners at the Savoy Café, a half-hour away, into the very core of hot jazz.

Looking at the books before me, I knew at last that I was not going to be a professor of American Studies—my major. I'd have to find a vocation where the continually unexpected was the norm. It couldn't be jazz because my clarinet playing wouldn't get me a gig anywhere. But jazz would help me find a way to my calling.

Leaving Harvard, never to return, I certified my emancipation by rushing to the Savoy and experiencing head-on what British critic Max Harrison called Bechet's "combination of violence and sensuous beauty"—an overwhelming emotional force, melodically and rhythmically, that stayed in the mind long after the night was over.

Starting when I was eleven, jazz musicians were the adults I most admired, even more than Ted Williams and some of his colleagues on the Boston Red Sox. Their music so lifted me up that at times, I'd shout in pleasure and surprise, even though I was a relatively proper Boston boy who did not ordinarily disturb the public peace.

Looking older than my age, I had gone to hear these musicians—including such visiting legends as Sidney Bechet and Wild Bill Davison—in clubs on Sunday afternoons and sometimes, unbeknownst to my parents, long into the night. At 19, I got to know many because I interviewed them on my jazz radio program on WMEX in Boston, and also broadcast remotes from the Savoy and later Storyville, another Boston jazz club.

Some of them became my graduate school faculty, where I was a perpetual student, listening them tell personal stories of Jim Crow that I hadn't heard about in courses at Boston Latin School, and also describe the countries and people they'd experienced in engagements in Europe and other continents.

And I measured the other adults I knew against these musicians' resilience of spirit. They made their living as improvisers, taking chances in public every night. Challenging themselves was their natural way of life.

Later, I found similar directness of speech and feeling among other creators of what Alan Lomax called "the rainbow of American music"—Merle Haggard, Willie Nelson, Charlie Rich, and Delbert McClinton, among them.

As a journalist, I've spent considerable time with, and admired, certain politicians; judges, even a Supreme Court justice; homicide detectives; defense lawyers; direct-action pacifists; writers; paladins of civil rights and civil liberties; and public school teachers who refused to let any child fail.

But by and large, when I'm not working, I most enjoy the company of the range of musicians in this book. Duke Ellington once wrote a song with the provocative title, "What I Am Here For?" The searchers in this book found out long ago, and with that essential knowledge as a foundation, they're free to keep exploring themselves through what they tell us in their music.

Trumpeter Clark Terry once said of Duke Ellington: "He wants life and music to be always in a state of becoming. He doesn't even like to write definitive endings to a piece. He'd often ask us to come up with ideas for closings, but when he'd settled on one of them, he'd keep fooling with it. He always likes to make the end of a song sound as if it's still going somewhere."

It's their constant state of becoming that draws me to people I write about, especially those who make music that I can hear whenever I need to connect again to the life force of these sounds of direct experience.

—NAT HENTOFF

THE JAZZ VOICE

Billie Holiday:
The Ghosts of "Strange Fruit"

On May 1, an exhibition on the history of lynching opened at the National Park Service's Martin Luther King Jr. National Historical Site in Atlanta. At its frightening center is "Without Sanctuary"—photographs taken at lynchings from the 1880s through the 1940s. It will be in Atlanta through the rest of the year.

As reported on National Public Radio, "the entrance to the exhibit is a small black room with a series of bright white lights. Words to the poem 'Strange Fruit' are printed on a wall in stark white letters. A recording of Billie Holiday's version of the ballad plays in the background. . . . This kind of detailed exhibit never has been shown in the South where a majority of lynchings took place."

James Allen, an antiques dealer in Atlanta, collected the photographs, but until now, he was never able to find a museum in the city—as the *Atlanta Journal-Constitution* notes—that was willing to display the pictures.

As Billie sings of "black bodies swinging in the Southern breeze, strange fruit hanging from the poplar trees," Jim Auchmutey of the *Constitution* wrote: "Viewers will

3

see the bodies of Laura Nelson and her son, L.W., dangling from a bridge in Oklahoma [and] the blistered flesh of a mentally retarded teenager burned alive before a crowd in Waco, Texas. In many of the photos, the white faces of lynchers and onlookers smile into the camera as if they were posing with trophy fish." Randall Burkett, an archivist at Emory University, says, "Nothing can make white folks appreciate the reality of racism in America like standing in a room with these images."

During the opening of "Without Sanctuary," Coretta Scott King said: "A great-uncle of mine was lynched in Alabama. I've heard about it all my life, and I'd like to know more." Another witness, Mary G. Johnson of Decatur, Alabama, told the *Atlanta Journal-Constitution* that a few years ago, she had visited Gorée Island, where generations of Africans had been forced into slave ships. "I didn't think," she said, "I could ever see anything worse than the Door of No Return. This is worse." A tour guide, taking her hand, asked, "Are you OK?" Mary Johnson could not answer.

Joseph Jordan, curator of the exhibit, wanted those photographs to speak directly to whites as well as blacks. "We have been the kind of society," he said, "that has studied the victims more than the perpetrators. I think it's about time now that we begin to look at some of the perpetrators." Along with Billie Holiday's singing, there are sounds of the woods at night, where many lynchings took place. And pictures—NPR's Kathy Lohr reported— "capture the faces of people leering or smiling during lynchings."

In conjunction with the exhibit of the photographs, there is a showing of Joel Katz's masterful documentary film, *Strange Fruit*, which covers: the history of the song; Billie Holiday's recording and other performances of it; commentary by, among others, Abbey Lincoln, Amina and Amiri Baraka, Milt Gabler (who recorded "Strange Fruit" for his Commodore label in 1939); and new information about the composer, Abel Meeropol. The score is by Don Byron.

Billie's "Strange Fruit" was not allowed on radio for some time, although I played it on my jazz radio program on Boston's WMEX in the mid-1940s. (The boss never listened to jazz.) Even without airplay, word-of-mouth was so effective that—as the film points out—the recording of "Strange Fruit" reached "Number 16 on the popular music charts only three months after its release. This was an unusually high ranking for a song which was banned by radio stations."

In the documentary there is a powerful performance of the song by Josh White. On being hauled before a House Unamerican Activities Committee's dragnet probe of Communist infiltration among blacks, White read the lyrics of "Strange Fruit," resulting in the subversive song appearing in the *Congressional Record*. (The Joel Katz documentary is available from California Newsreel, www.newsreel.org; phone: 415-284-7800, with special pricing for high schools, public libraries, and community groups.)

The film ends with an intriguing performance of "Strange Fruit" by Cassandra Wilson, but it's eclipsed by an earlier BBC appearance by Billie in 1959. This was the last time she performed the song before she died in July of that year. That performance is available on *The Billie Holiday Set* on the Toronto-based Baldwin Street Music label (www.baldwinstreetmusic.com). The set also contains several interviews with Billie.

At the end of the Joel Katz documentary film, Pete Seeger says: "People have tried to explain in words what the power of music is—and usually failed. All we know is that sometimes, a short song, taking just a few minutes, can have as much impression on a listener as sometimes a whole novel can. . . . You can bounce the experiences of your life against it, and it bounces back new meanings."

At the "Without Sanctuary" exhibit, seventy-year-old John Crawford is reading an NAACP pamphlet, in a glass case, describing the lynching of a black farmer, his grandfather, Anthony Crawford, in Abbeville, South Carolina, in 1916. He tells a reporter from the *Constitution*: "I've got some sons who need to look at this," as he touches the glass tenderly.

BILLIE HOLIDAY:
LADY DAY—ALL THE WAY

B illie Holiday's impact on other jazz musicians, as well as listeners, was once described by the trumpet player Roy Eldridge: "Billie must have come from another world because nobody had the effect on people she had. She could really get to people. I've seen her make them cry and make them happy."

And her favorite accompanist, pianist Bobby Tucker, added: "It was a thrill to play for her. She had the greatest conception of a beat I ever heard. She could sing the fastest tune or something that was like a dirge, and she'd be right there. With Lady, you could relax while you were playing for her. . . . With most singers you have to guide them and carry them along."

Lady Day was the name tenor saxophonist Lester Young gave her, and she called him "Pres" (for president of the saxophone), and that's how both were referred to by their peers. I once asked her about her influences. "I always try to sing like a horn," she said. "A trumpet or a tenor saxophone, like Lester."

Later, interviewed by Willis Conover on the Voice of America, Billie said, "I've always liked the big sound that

Bessie Smith got, but when I was quite young, I heard Louis Armstrong's 'West End Blues.' He doesn't sing any words on it, but I liked the wonderful feeling he got. He sounded like he was making love to you. I didn't have a big voice, but between the two of them, I sort of got Billie Holiday."

Billie seldom sang the blues in its traditional forms, but its textures were in her improvising. "The blues," she told me, "is like being very sad, very sick, going to church, being very happy. And when I sing, it's never the same way twice. It's just according to how I feel. Anything I sing, it's part of my life."

Billie Holiday died in 1959. She was forty-four. Her recordings continue to be reissued in various formats because, never having been concerned with fashion, she has never been out of fashion. There is now a 10-CD box set, *Lady Day: The Complete Billie Holiday (1933–1944)* on Columbia/Legacy. Actually, the 230 tracks include all the masters released and unreleased in the United States on the Columbia, Brunswick, Vocalion, Okeh, and Harmony labels, plus radio air-checks. There are also extensive biographical and discographical notes, but I would suggest postponing those for a long winter night. Just listen to Billie.

Starting with her first recording with Benny Goodman (1933), which she later wished had never been issued ("I sound like I'm about three years old"), the enormous set ranges through the legendary Teddy Wilson sides with Lester Young, Roy Eldridge, Johnny Hodges, and brief appearances with Count Basie and Duke Ellington, among other sessions.

Billie, on and off stage, had a quick, ironic wit. One night, at the home of a mutual friend, I heard her satirical impressions of various self-important bookers and managers in the jazz business. And I can easily imagine her reaction to this lavish presentation of these famous eleven years of her recording career.

"I made over 200 sides between 1933 and 1944," she said in the book *Lady Sings the Blues*, "but I don't get a cent of royalties on any of them. They paid me twenty-five, fifty or a top of seventy-five bucks a side, and I was glad to get it. . . . But royalties were still unheard of."

For quite a time thereafter, royalties continued to be scarce for jazz sidemen and singers. When I was reporting on the scene full time in the 1950s and 1960s, musicians would tell me, "All I get, and all I expect, is what I get for the date."

The promotional material for this invaluable collection does echo a judgment by many—though not all—jazz critics that those eleven years were, "by all observances, her most important phase as a recording artist." In her later years, it is conventionally said, Billie—struggling with addiction to drugs and a most unfortunate choice of men—was not up to the often ebullient and always compelling performances of her youth. Of these men, Billie reminisced, "I was as strong if not stronger than any of them. When it's that way, you can't blame anybody but yourself."

Throughout her career, I heard her as often as I could, and during the 1950s, there were indeed nights when her voice and her spirit cracked. But at other times—and even when she was in twilight—her voice, darker and deeper, still held an audience. As Miles Davis told me, "You know, she's not thinking now what she was in 1937. She still has control, probably more control now than then."

And Benny Green, the British jazz musician, who became a consistently astute writer on the music, said of her last recordings, "They are not the insufferable croakings of a woman already half dead but . . . statements as frank and tragic as anything throughout the whole range of popular art."

But during the last decade of her life, there are also recordings by her in high spirits and with the same resilient jazz time and authority that Carmen McRae— whose singing Billie nurtured—described: "Singing is the only place she can express herself the way she'd like to be all the time."

Just as essential as the Columbia/Legacy recordings of the 1933–1944 Holiday is *The Billie Holiday Set: A Midsummer Night's Jazz at Stratford '57* (Baldwin Street Music, www.baldwinstreetmusic.com). These twenty-two tracks include not only a program at the Stratford Shakespeare Festival in Ontario but also *A Portrait of Lady 1945–1959*, with live performances in Los Angeles, at the Apollo Theater in New York, and television appearances climaxed by a February 24, 1959, performance of "Strange Fruit" on the BBC in which she was accompanied only by the pianist Mal Waldron. It was the last time she sang that threnody of the years of lynching, and it is searing. It illustrates Benny Green's assessment of her last years. There are also several interviews with Billie.

Baldwin Street Music, located in Toronto, is the creation of Ted Ono, who brings back to life rare recordings of singers whom he cherishes. In his notes to *The Billie Holiday Set,* Mr. Ono writes that when Billie died in a hospital on July 17, 1959, "She had no money in her bank account. All she had was a bunch of hundred-dollar bills wrapped around her thigh with a garter belt."

But she left a legacy unmatched in the history of jazz.

Ivie Anderson:
For the Love of Ivie

I was talking with Duke Ellington in his dressing room when a slender, vivid, angry spirit swept in. It was Ivie Anderson, who had a grievance, which she expressed in remarkably inventive, salty language until she took note of me, stopped and vanished.

Characteristically unruffled, Duke continued our conversation. I wished she had stayed so I could have told her how often I played "Rose of the Rio Grande," with Ivie and Lawrence Brown gamboling through the band. And when I was lonely, I'd sought companionship in her sensuous interplay with Johnny Hodges in "Rocks in My Bed."

Ellington had three particularly distinctive singers. Adelaide Hall—as in the 1927 "Creole Love Call"—was really another instrument in her wordless vocals, which sometimes became the kind of evocative growls in which Bubber Miley, and later Cootie Williams, also specialized. And Kay Davis—with, as Ira Gitler put it, her "almost ethereal" soprano—delighted Duke as he wove her wordless sounds into the ensemble.

But it was Ivie whom Duke regarded as the vocalist who best embodied the band's resilient spirit. As Harry

Carney, Duke's baritone saxophonist—and driver on the road—described her: on stage, "she looked angelic and above it all, yet backstage and on the bus, hotels, and restaurants, everywhere she was always regular 100 percent. There was no side [pretentiousness] to her." Ivie was much more than a girl singer. She was a sidewoman.

The Harry Carney quote is from Sally-Ann Worsfold's scrupulously researched notes to *Raisin' the Rent*, the first of two volumes of *Ivie Anderson with Duke Ellington's Orchestra*. The second is *All God's Chillun*. The performances are from 1932 to 1937, as lovingly—I do not exaggerate—put together by Alistair Robertson, a jazz enthusiast and owner of Hep Records in Edinburgh, Scotland.

Ivie Anderson, born in a Los Angeles suburb in 1905, had been with various West Coast bands; worked as a dancer and singer in a vaudeville troupe headed by Mamie Smith; and sang with Earl Hines, where Duke heard and hired her in 1931. Asthma forced her to retire eleven years later, and she died in 1948.

Watching movie classics on television, you might see her in the Marx Brothers' *A Day at the Races*, in which Ivie was cast as a washerwoman. But as Sally-Ann Worsfold writes, Ivie blithely transcended that role and the script: "In one of her most vivacious, jubilant appearances, a radiant Ivie, in Pied Piper fashion, is joined by a group of African-American children" followed by Harpo Marx, "blowing a penny whistle."

Ivie had an unerring sense of jazz time. Her phrasing was so musicianly that she fitted seamlessly into the band, and she had as strong a presence as the famed soloists in the orchestra. Ivie became the lyrics, and her multitextured sound adapted easefully to the wide-ranging spectrum of Duke's compositions.

In these recordings on the Hep label, Ivie exemplified "It Don't Mean a Thing," and her contribution to "Solitude" was deeper than that of anyone else I've heard who ever sang it. She got into equivalents of characters in short stories through such haunting numbers as "Troubled Waters," "In a Mizz," and a "Stormy Weather" that even eclipsed Ethel Water's way with that Harold Arlen song. When Ivie introduced the number to British audiences, she—as Duke recalled—would "stop the show cold."

Ivie also appears in the justly treasured three-disc Duke Ellington *The Blanton-Webster Band* (Bluebird/RCA) in, among other tracks, "Rocks in My Bed" and "I Got It Bad (and that Ain't Good"), the latter also in intimate consonance with Johnny Hodges.

Ivie always brings me out of the blues with her singing of "Rose of the Rio Grande" and "All God's Chillun" on the Hep Records CD.

Like Billie Holiday, Ivie, even with Duke, at times had to deal with what used to be called "dog tunes"—with apologies to my Samoyed, Lulu. But she could make even "Swingtime in Honolulu" and "Love Is Like a Cigarette" listenable. But fortunately, the two Hep sets include "Ebony Rhapsody," "Mood Indigo," and others worthy of her and Duke. Ivie was so vivid I can still see her storming into Duke's dressing room.

TEDDY GRACE:
A JOYFUL REUNION WITH THE
BLUES OF TEDDY GRACE

first heard Elvis Presley before I knew his name. It was
on a pop music radio station and I couldn't understand
why it was playing Big Boy Crudup, a black Mississippi blues singer. But it was Elvis, and I later learned he
had studied up on Mr. Crudup. This was long before Elvis
became an icon.

Back then Elvis could speak the blues, but few whites
have been able to. One was Jack Teagarden, whose voice
and trombone were all of one piece. Another was Teddy
Grace from Arcadia, Louisiana. Born in 1905 as Stella
Gloria Crowson, she insisted on being called Teddy as
soon as she could insist, and her last name changed
through various marriages.

She made a few records with dance bands, but it was a
1939 Decca album, *Blues Sung by Teddy Grace*, that
brought her to the attention of serious blues and jazz collectors. And they were serious back then, pouring over
genealogies as well as styles. But Teddy Grace came from
the wrong side of the blues tracks. She was white, her

family was more than comfortable; and Teddy had picked up an abiding interest in the blues from blacks who worked in her home.

When that Decca blues album came out, however, a lot of jukebox listeners and record buyers thought she was black. Unlike Elvis's imitation of Big Boy Crudup, Teddy Grace didn't try to imitate black bards. But her natural warmth and powerful, easeful rhythmic flow made her sound as if she knew their language from the inside. She sang the blues—and some jazz—with such appealing self-assurance that it didn't matter what side of the tracks she'd come from. She was riding the train.

The musicians on that date—trombonist Sonny Lee, Charlie Shavers on trumpet, and pianist Billy Kyle—knew they weren't dealing with a beginner in the blues and jazz. Teddy Grace ran the session, and her singing convinced them she had a right to.

Teddy Grade made her last recordings in 1940 with, among other singular improvisers, clarinetist Pee Wee Russell and tenor saxophonist Bug Freeman. Then, at age thirty-five, she disappeared from the music scene.

I kept her 78 rpm Decca blues album for years, until it disappeared too. And I asked anyone I could, including European collectors, if they knew where she had gone. Eventually, I figured she was probably dead. Still, I kept asking, and one day I got a call from David McCain, another ardent admirer of her singing.

She had indeed died, in 1992, but before then McCain had interviewed her a number of times, and he'd also talked to members of her family and musicians who had played with her. He also found all of her recordings. McCain's account of the ascent and disappearance of Teddy Grace are contained in a Timeless Records CD, *Teddy Grace* (available in many Tower Records stores and directly from the Village Jazz Shop in New York).

Teddy Grace told McCain that she had abandoned the music business out of frustration. She was weary of battling with Decca over the songs she wanted to record, and, like most performers in all fields, she blamed the company for insufficiently vigorous promotion of her work.

She joined the Women's Army Corps; became a successful recruiter, surpassing quotas; and with her customary enthusiasm organized shows for the Service Command in Texas and Arkansas. In 1944, she completely lost her voice, ascribing it to exhaustion. And although it gradually came back, she was never able to sing again.

For a long time, she worked as a statistical typist at Rockwell International, a rather unusual day job for a blues singer, or maybe not. David McCain found her in 1991 in a suburban Los Angeles nursing home. Teddy Grace had cancer.

"She was very flattered to be remembered," he writes. "Very sweet and gracious. . . . She had no idea that she was a mystery figure and that many people over the years had wondered whatever happened to her."

As McCain notes, her recordings "were still on 78 rpm records, either hidden away in private collections or gathering dust in second-hand stores all over the world."

Rescued by Timeless Records, there are twenty-two tracks. Of primary interest are all thirteen of her blues recordings. Timeless is the word. I have never heard Teddy Grace in a club or a ballroom, but these have the immediacy and exhilaration of live performances. The music stalks through the night—"Down Home Blues," "You Don't Know My Mind," "Gulf Coast Blues," "Hey Lawdy Papa."

Forever in her thirties, Teddy Grace keeps talking the blues:

> "I went to the graveyard and fell down on my knees,
> I asked that old gravedigger to give me back my good man
>   please . . .
> The man I love got a mouthful of gold,
> Every time he kisses me, makes my blood run cold . . .
> From now on, daddy, I'm going to be all for myself."

ABBEY LINCOLN:
GOD BLESS THE CHILD
THAT HAS HER OWN

I have known jazz originals whose music over the years has dramatically evolved—notably that of the tenor saxophonist John Coltrane. But Abbey Lincoln, like Coltrane, is one of the few to have also deeply changed in their personal lives in ways that affected their music. Such a transformation will be in evidence when Jazz at Lincoln Center presents "Abbey Lincoln: Over the Years—An Anthology of Her Songs," a three-day retrospective that begins on Thursday.

I first recorded her on the drummer Max Roach's album *We Insist! Freedom Now Suite* (Candid), which was regarded as the earliest full-scale protest record in jazz when it was released in 1960. By then, Lincoln had already changed from her previous manifestation as an alluring supper-club singer, working rooms like Ciro's in Los Angeles and the Club Elegante in Brooklyn. "They put me in a Marilyn Monroe-type dress," she recalled disdainfully, "and I sang the more titillating standards and phony folk tunes, and they told me 'not to sound like a Negro.' "

Deciding she no longer wanted to be a "shallow woman featuring her breasts," Ms. Lincoln was wearing her hair "natural" by 1958 and had become engaged in the civil rights movement. Her liberation as a singer came about through her meeting and subsequent marriage to Mr. Roach. He helped her learn new harmonic progressions and persuaded her to throw the Monroe-style dress in the incinerator.

Although she had recorded with jazz musicians for a few years before the *Freedom Now Suite*, it brought her widespread attention, not all of it favorable. The work encompassed slavery to emancipation to the civil rights movement. It also included a fierce denunciation of apartheid ("Tears for Johannesburg"). The musicians—the magisterial Coleman Hawkins among them—played passionately, but the most startling section was "Protest," featuring ordered, wordless screaming by Ms. Lincoln.

All of us involved were elated when the *Freedom Now Suite* was banned in South Africa. But we were soon angered when her next recording for Candid, *Straight Ahead*, which I also produced, received a review in *Down Beat* magazine, in which she was called "a professional Negro." The reviewer, Ira Gitler, added: "We don't need the Elijah Muhammad type of thinking in jazz."

The album brought to a boil racial divisions that had long existed in jazz. Some black musicians contended that they essentially owned jazz and that it was being stolen from them by whites. White musicians complained that they were the victims of Crow Jim, reverse discrimination. Miles Davis took a lot of heat from black musicians when he hired the white pianist Bill Evans for his combo. But as Davis told me at the time, "I don't care if he's purple with green dots so long as he can play."

In response to the release of *Freedom Now Suite,* Mr. Roach, Ms. Lincoln, and I participated in a lively discussion on "Racial Prejudice in Jazz" held at the offices of *Down Beat,* which later published a transcript. Also on the panel were a number of offended white jazz critics, including Mr. Gitler, and the musicians Don Ellis and Lalo Schifrin. There was little consonance. "Everybody bleeds," Ms. Lincoln said at one point. "But people are not the same. Their environment and experiences make them different."

As for whether race pride was synonymous with racism, Ms. Lincoln asked, "Why is that because I love my people and I want human dignity must I be a racist?"

The racial tension in jazz has lessened considerably over the last four decades, though not disappeared entirely. During a panel discussion on whether jazz should be defined as black music at the San Francisco Jazz Festival last year, Steve Coleman, a black alto saxophonist who will perform at the Lincoln retrospective, repeated an often heard refrain: that he could always tell on listening to a recording whether the musician was black or white. I reminded him that the legendary black trumpet player Roy Eldridge had once made the same claim, but that in a famous blindfold test conducted by *Down Beat,* he had been wrong more than half the time.

Over the years, Ms. Lincoln turned her attention to songwriting and composing. She says she was greatly encouraged by the praise she received from Thelonious Monk for her lyrics to his composition "Blue Monk." She also became a compelling actress, appearing in the films *Nothing but a Man* (1964) and *For Love of Ivy* (1968), in which she starred with Sidney Poitier. Ms. Lincoln said he was surprised that she had been given the part "after all the screaming and hollering I did on the *'Freedom Now Suite.'''*

The two recordings she made for Candid, however, were regarded as so controversial that after Candid went out of business not long after she released *Straight Ahead* in 1961, she was not asked to make another recording for ten years.

Then, she said, she was approached by Jean-Phillipe Allard of the French label Verve Gitanes, for which she recorded the albums *You Gotta Pay the Band, A Turtle's Dream,* and *Who Used to Dance.* Other recordings for the label followed. In reviewing her 1998 album *Wholly Earth* in *The Penguin Guide to Jazz on CD,* Richard Cook and Brian Morton describe her voice as being "so confidently intimate, so easily conversational, that it becomes difficult to think of Lincoln in terms of 'performance.' " They also wrote of "her ability to make large harmonic shifts and to reshuffle tempos."

Ms. Lincoln has told Ingrid Monson, professor of Afro-American Studies and Music at Harvard University: "I don't scream any more. I sing about my life. I feel accomplished because I've learned to be a writer. I sing the songs I write. I don't sing anybody else's material for the most part except for some old standards."

She also writes plays and has written extensively on Africa and Egypt. As for her view of herself in the world, Ms. Lincoln said recently: "we are all human beings, some of us with lighter or darker skins. We can make a baby with anybody on the planet."

In a talk delivered at a symposium in honor of Ms. Lincoln at Columbia University in December, Ms. Monson quoted Ms. Lincoln: "I've lost any preference for anybody. Everybody looks the same to me now. I look at the human being and I see myself. I'm not only African. I represent the human being."

I was once asked during a BBC program on Ms. Lincoln how I would characterize her. "She has an integrity," I said, "that can cut your head off."

Frank Sinatra:
Sinatra in Paris
with Small Combo, 1962

One afternoon, I went to a Frank Sinatra rehearsal at the Copacabana in New York. Waiting for the music to start, I read the paper until a muscular resident Yahoo growled that no reading was permitted in the club at any time. Demanding a reason, I was answered with a glare that ended the conversation. But then Sinatra arrived, and my glowering about the venue he'd picked stopped.

There was a large orchestra, and from time to time, Sinatra conducted it. During an intricately lyrical passage, Sinatra stopped the music. "That was a B natural you just played," he said to a trombonist. "Look at the score. It should have been a B flat."

I later told Gene Lees, the singer-critic, that I hadn't known Sinatra had that good an ear beyond his own singing. Lees told of the time Sinatra conducted some pieces by Alex Wilder who was asked, "Did Sinatra really conduct that music?" Wilder answered that Sinatra had conducted those pieces better than anyone else, all the more "because he understands dance tempos."

A few months ago, I was talking to Ron Anthony, a guitarist who has been with the Sinatra road show since 1986. "His sense of swing," Anthony said, "is just fantastic. When he's in a groove, he reminds me of such swinging tenor saxophonists as Zoot Sims and Stan Getz. And his phrasing is part of that groove."

While I've heard Sinatra in various settings through the years, I've often wondered what he would sound like with a small jazz combo that could spur him to stretch out. With a big band or a large orchestra, a singer is cushioned by the arrangements. But with a small combo, the singer can't hide.

Reprise has issued just such a highly informal Sinatra session recorded live in Paris in 1962. For Sinatra's debut in that city, he played the Lido, a big Champs-Elysees nightclub. The band he chose to bring, however, was neither big nor brassy. Pianist Bill Miller was the musical director, and the rest of the instrumentation consisted of vibes, guitar, bass, drums and multi-reedman Harry Klee.

In his previous outings, with the bands of Harry James and Tommy Dorsey, Sinatra projected a self-assurance that was sometimes abrasively cocky, although on ballads, he sounded autobiographically vulnerable. In *Sinatra in Paris*, the self-assurance is warmly collegial, like an after-hours session. I have never heard Sinatra so relaxed and buoyant, with such an infectious and swinging beat.

One of the sidemen on this date, guitarist Al Viola, told James Isaacs, who wrote the illuminating liner notes, that there are times when Sinatra sounded "almost like an instrument. The guys in the band thought of Frank as our tenor man."

All twenty-five songs in the set are standards. Sinatra likes the familiar—in part to keep challenging himself to create variations on the lyrics and the structure of the song. Here, for instance, he recharges "Moonlight in Vermont," "Night and Day," and many other perennials with phrasing that brings new light to old expectations.

He even makes "Ol' Man River" an extension of his own life and times. As James Isaacs notes: "That a multi-millionaire white entertainer would dare attempt to portray a black stevedore . . . during the present era of heightened racial awareness and sensitivity may seem foolhardy at best. But Sinatra's 'River' is as much the Hudson (in New Jersey) as the Mississippi."

Sinatra grew up "among the dock wallopers of Hoboken," and makes this "an immigrant's tale" as a corollary to the black experience in the South. One way he does this is by not trying to sound at all black.

Even now, when he sometimes forgets the lyrics and looks his age as he sings from memory of the rehearsals of love, there are bursts of exhilaration as he connects with the internal resident musician who has yet to abandon him. The extraordinary pleasure of this discovery of Sinatra in Paris thirty-four years ago is that his high spirits, his manifest delight in surprising himself, course through just about every track, from "I've Got You Under My Skin" and "In The Still of the Night" to "I Could Have Danced All Night" and "Come Fly with Me."

Sinatra has a section to himself in the extensive *New Grove Dictionary of Jazz.* In the entry, Henry Pleasants, who didn't have a chance to hear the Paris set, writes that "Sinatra is best known as a popular singer, but he is nevertheless highly respected in jazz circles, above all for his relaxed and subtle sense of swing."

Ron Anthony, Sinatra's current guitarist, has worked with jazz groups and singers and says that he still listens carefully to the seventy-nine-year-old swinger because of Sinatra's sense of time. Sinatra is not likely to get off the road as long as he can move. If he were to stop performing, time would stop.

FRED ASTAIRE:
SOME SINGING—AND HOOFING—
WITH THE BOYS

The late Norman Granz became reasonably wealthy through the jazz concerts he organized and promoted throughout the world. But he recorded on his various labels primarily those musicians and singers he particularly enjoyed, with little concern for sales figures. Once, at a meeting with his distributor, Granz was asked why he kept performers who sold only a few thousand copies a year. "If only a few thousand people want to hear them," Granz said, "they should be able to." And—he later told me—he fired the distributor.

As in his "Jazz at the Philharmonic" concerts, Granz often gathered musicians of varying styles, so long as they knew how to swing. In 1952, he persuaded Fred Astaire to record a session with a small jazz combo. Granz felt Astaire's mastery of rhythms could extend to jazz time. And when I've been asked to define jazz singing, aside from listing the obvious names I suggest trying to find *The Astaire Story* (Verve).

On the two-CD set, Granz chose musicians at ease in a range of settings: pianist Oscar Peterson, tenor saxophonist Flip Phillips, Charlie Shavers on trumpet, guitarist Barney Kessel, Ray Brown on bass, and Alvin Stoller on drums. There were no rehearsals and no written arrangements. Astaire and the players talked about each song, worked out the sequence and, as Astaire says in the notes, "Some we got on the first take, and some of them—well, a little longer."

By contrast with the carefully constructed, self-conscious attempts at swinging by such current "jazz" divas as Diana Krall and Jane Monheit, Astaire, without any guideposts but his own instincts and imagination, became one of the swinging improvisers on the date. "A sort of new addition," as he puts it, "to the Jazz at the Philharmonic group."

In his recent book, *A Jazz Odyssey* (Continuum), which is full of inside stories, Oscar Peterson notes: "For all his rhythmic feel, Fred was not naturally attuned to jazz phrasing. . . . Dancing, his time was so strict that he could make an accompaniment sound early or late; his vocal time, however, was very loose, uninhibited and unmeasured. I found the best way to accompany him was to give him a long harmonic chord-cushion and let him take his natural liberties with metronomic time."

What comes through is the spontaneous pleasure of the musicians and Astaire as they kept finding a common groove, using space as an integral, moving part of each number. At the end of his notes on the session, Astaire writes: "To say that I got my kicks out of doing this job is putting it mildly indeed." Once attuned to the other improvisers, Astaire was jubilant in discovering how loosely swinging he could be.

You can also hear Astaire's footwork on the disks. He describes those tracks as "doing some hoofing with the boys." And the tap-dance breaks—when only he is heard—are jazz breaks. As Oscar Peterson writes, "these [dance] tracks were not easy to do . . . they eventually came off, and I treasure them as genuine musical moments rather than any kind of intriguing oddity."

One of the reasons Granz wanted to record Astaire was, as he told Peterson, because "Not too many people realized how many of our great standards were either introduced by Fred or centrally featured in his movies."

Included in the twenty-eight tracks are: "Isn't This a Lovely Day," "S Wonderful," "The Way You Look Tonight," "Dancing in the Dark," "Night and Day," "They Can't Take That Away From Me," and "Oh, Lady Be Good." Of that last song, Astaire says, "I don't think George [Gershwin] ever thought 'Lady Be Good' would become a jazz classic."

Among his informal spoken introductions, there is: "Of all the songs I've done, I think this next one is the nearest thing to a trademark. I'm particularly fond of this old fellow. When Irving Berlin wrote it for me, I found it a real inspiration: 'Top Hat, White Tie and Tails.'"

As a ballad singer Astaire—in "I Concentrate on You," "Dancing in the Dark"—is naturally, romantically intimate, the mood illuminated by the lyrical coloration of his jazz colleagues.

Charlie Shavers, only glancingly mentioned these days by jazz critics, was an original, both as a shouter and in reflective choruses such as these accompanying Astaire. Flip Phillips is mostly remembered for his explosive battles with other horns on "Jazz at the Philharmonic" stages, but his tenderness is movingly consonant with Astaire's.

A surprise in the set is Astaire, the pianist, in a song he co-wrote, "Not My Girl." He says, "Piano playing is a serious hobby of mine, and still is. So you know, I was bound to sneak it in here somewhere. I'll start out by playing the first chorus in the same style I used, then Oscar rescues me and takes it from there." Astaire sounds like he's inside a player piano, but there's a rollicking jazz touch to the jollity, and more of it in the singing, as Astaire struts to Peterson's bravura accompaniment that sounds, as he often does, as if he has three hands.

"Jazz means the blues," Astaire says in introducing "Slow Dances," adding: "Oscar, Barney, Alvin, and Ray are going to ad lib some of those blues, and I'm going to walk in and throw a little hoofing in there." During these basic blues, Astaire taps crisply and authoritatively in the front line.

On July 1, in the New York Post, Pete Hamill, in a patriotic mode, recalled that in Rome, "a bitter expatriate" had asked him if he loved his country and if so to provide a reason why. Hamill answered: "Fred Astaire . . . He epitomized the virtues of a free country, with his grace and elegance, his humor and his ease, and his utter lack of vanity . . . No other nation could have produced him."

And since no other nation could have produced jazz, Norman Granz was right in arranging a jazz gig for Fred Astaire.

THE BLUES

You Heard It Here First:
When the Sun Goes Down

I n the early 1950s, as I noted, listening to a radio station that programmed Perry Como, Patti Page, and other pop music favorites, I was startled to hear the black Mississippi blues singer Arthur "Big Boy" Crudup. Or so I thought. The disc jockey, however, after the driving rhythms of "That's All Right" had ended, announced the first recording by Elvis Presley.

This white Mississippian, I found out, had been strongly influenced by Crudup and recorded two other songs by him. As blues historian Salvatore Caputo noted, "That's All Right" became "the catalyst of the rock 'n' roll explosion of the 1950s," presaging the pervasive influence of the blues on Bob Dylan, the Grateful Dead, and legions of other singers and instrumentalists on the hit charts since.

The impact of the blues on what the late folklorist Alan Lomax called the "rainbow of American music" is wondrously illuminated in a newly released four-CD set, *When the Sun Goes Down: The Secret History of Rock & Roll*—100 tracks from the archives of the RCA Victor and Bluebird labels (1920s to 1950s). (Each one of the four CDs is currently available for $13.98. The box set will sell in stores for $55.98.)

"Big Boy" Crudup is here, along with such classic blues singers and instrumentalists as Blind Willie McTell, Sonny Boy Williamson, Leroy Carr, Tampa Red, Sleepy John Estes, Gus Cannon's Jug Stompers, and many more. These are not dusty, scratchy performances of interest only to specialists in the genre. They are as immediately vivid and resonating as when they were first released, primarily to black audiences. The remarkably clear sound quality is a tribute to audio engineer Doug Pomeroy and co-producer Barry Feldman, who found original metal masters, test pressings, and mint condition 78s borrowed from collectors. I bought some of these when they first came out, and they sound much better now.

In addition to hearing the specific sources for later hit recordings by the Rolling Stones, Eric Clapton, Chuck Berry, Hank Williams, Ray Charles, Van Morrison, Willie Nelson, the Allman Brothers, and many others, listeners are presented with a wide-ranging, intriguingly anecdotal history of the blues itself. The notes by roots-music historian Colin Escott and David Evans, a University of Memphis professor of ethnomusicology, reflect, in tone and style, the pleasurable immersion of the writers.

Even long-term listeners to the blues are likely to make some discoveries. On the third volume, "That's Chicago's South Side," for example, Robert Nighthawk (born Robert McCollum), bursts through—in "Prowling Night Hawk"—as a storyteller of uncommon power. He had a couple of hits decades ago, but he didn't follow up because, the notes explain, "he traveled compulsively" and "many claimed his acquaintance; few knew him."

Much better known, though hardly a household word these days, is Jimmie Rodgers, billed as "the singing brakeman" from his railroad days. He appears in the second volume, "The First Time I Met the Blues," and also in my recommendation as a print companion volume to this audio-history, Bill Malone's revised *Country Music USA* (University of Texas Press), the best single introduction to piebald country music. Rodgers, "father of country music," as Mr. Malone calls him, was connected to black music. Years ago, on a field recording of tribal African songs in a remote village, I heard a tribute to him, by name, including his "blue yodel." Here he is accompanied by cornetist Louis Armstrong, a blues master.

Wholly new to me was Edna Winston in a 1927 Victor recording. Dramatic, but also poignant, her "Rent Man Blues" is shown as an example of why "she was an outstanding find for Victor Records," I'd like to hear much more of and about her, but her entry closes with "absolutely nothing is known of her."

In politics, as well as music, much was known of Jimmie Davis, twice the singing governor of Louisiana. Evans and Escott write that "he openly supported segregation, but began his career singing smutty blues with a true blues-man, Oscar Woods, on guitar." His political opponents used his crossing of the color line against him, "but it only increased his popularity." So did his attractive singing voice here in "Red Nightgown Blues" with Mr. Woods, whatever his political views, along for the gig.

A discovery for me on Volume Four, "That's All Right," was Peter Clayton (self-billed as Doctor Clayton), whom B.B. King—the sempiternal blues singer—idolized. ("Just about everything he did, I used to sing along with it.") Clayton was, we are told, "one of the finest songwriters in the history of the blues. He claimed to have been born in Africa, but it's likelier that his parents were from South Africa and that he was born in Georgia." The blues travel long and far.

One of his performances in this set, with "his strangled high-tenor," is "Angels in Harlem." Doctor Clayton knew of the blues: "He lost his wife and kids in a house fire, and died in 1947, never knowing how influential his writing or singing style would become."

Also on Volume Four is the song that propelled the career of Peggy Lee, "Why Don't You Do Right." But the singer here, Lil Green, accompanied by Big Bill Broonzy on guitar, died in 1954—having come to Chicago from Mississippi—with "little more" known about her now than "her several imperishable small-group classics."

The blues could be sorrowful, sometimes desperate, but also full of joyous anticipation—as in Tampa Red's "Sweet Little Angel" with its celebratory opening line: "I got a sweet little angel, and I love the way she spreads her wings."

Joe Williams:
He Brought the Blues from
the Country to the City

Some nights, during the 1950s, walking down the stairs to Birdland, billed as "the jazz center of the world," I had a sense of what it felt like to be in the face of a hurricane.

From below, the physical impact of the Count Basie band in full cry almost pushed me against the wall. And penetrating that swing machine was the soaring, diving, exultant voice of Joe Williams. As Cassandra Wilson says, Joe "brought the blues from the country to the city."

The deep cry of country blues blended seamlessly with Joe Williams' city-honed wit and hard-earned wisdom. He was a pleasure to talk to because he knew so much from his own life of what it took to more than survive. As a teenager, in between musical gigs, he cleaned latrines, worked as a stage doorman, and once went down so low it took a year in a state hospital after a nervous breakdown to make him stronger than ever before.

One night, in his dressing room, we were talking about musicians we knew who were in the grave or had slipped into oblivion, some of them having been their own worst enemy. Joe Williams pointed at me and said, "You and I are survivors!" That he considered me to be at all comparable to him in that regard was an honor. Whether in the blues or in ballads, Joe sang from his own life. Like Billie Holiday, he made the lyrics into intimations of autobiography. He'd been down as far as you can go and he'd risen as high as any jazz singer ever has.

Joe Williams was a thoughtful man, given to analyzing his art. And it was a high art. Ten years ago, speaking with Terry Gross during a *Fresh Air* show broadcast on National Public Radio, he got to the essence of authentic jazz singing: "If you sing like a musical instrument, you don't try to cover up your support. The music will swing if you try not to get in the way. The same is true of a drummer as a singer.

"You're the soloist, so you can punctuate, make a statement, but you don't get in the way of the music itself. And it gives everybody a chance to contribute. You mustn't ever have anyone in a section back there feeling, 'My part is not important.' All the parts are important; and if it's done subtly, I have to make room for it so that it's heard, and heard the way they want it to be heard."

Like many black jazz musicians, the first music Joe Williams heard was in church; and at fourteen, he was a member of the Jubilee Boys, a gospel quartet. His mother, a pianist and a singer, made sure the boy was also exposed to a wide range of music.

"She used to let me stay awake to listen to Duke Ellington in the 1930s broadcasting from the Cotton Club and then kiss me and tuck me in after the band went off." He was around eight when he first heard Louis Armstrong in a theater. Later, listening to Ethel Waters on the radio, he marveled at the clarity of her diction and the feeling, the worldly-wise feeling, with which she illuminated whatever she sang. And, like Coleman Hawkins, he'd learn from the larger-than-life opera singers on the radio.

Joe's commanding presence lit up huge concert halls, but I remember him with the most delight and gratitude for how he absorbed the emotions of his audience in a small club. Their shouts when he rode the blues and their sighs when he sang of fragile love came back into his singing. The day after Joe died, Bob Edwards, host of National Public Radio's *Morning Edition*, recalled going to see Joe in a small club in Maryland. It was the night of a Muhammad Ali fight on TV, "and Williams performed in front of just three couples, but he sang as if it was a packed house in Vegas." Among the current Telarc releases by Joe are *Joe Williams Live with the Count Basie Orchestra*; a set of ballads with Robert Farnon's orchestra, *Here's to Life*; and *Feel the Spirit*, in which Joe returns to his gospel roots with Marlena Shaw and a chorus.

Joe Williams survives as long as there is a need for music that tells a true story. All the times I saw and heard Joe on nights when he wasn't feeling all that good or when the band wasn't quite together, he never coasted, he never took the weight off himself. Like that night in Maryland, he was asked afterward, "With only three couples in the room, why didn't you come down with laryngitis? Tell them to come back another time." "No," said Joe, "the only real reward is when you've done the best you could. It isn't money all the time."

Jazz and Deep Jewish Blues

On trumpet, and as a composer and leader, Steven Bernstein is uncategorizable. (See his "Before and After" session with Bill Milkowski in the October, 2002 *JazzTimes*.) But Bernstein and I share roots in centuries-old Jewish soul music—the improvisations of the chazans, the cantors, in synagogues. (Or shuls, as they were called in my neighborhood.)

I have been waiting for Steven Bernstein's *Diaspora Blues* with the Sam Rivers trio for more than fifty years because it bridges the most personal and yet also cosmic way of answering Duke Ellington's question "What am I here for?" I used to tell Charles Mingus about Jewish blues and how they naturally flow into jazz, and I wish he were here to hear *Diaspora Blues*.

As a boy and after, I collected cantorial recordings, and among my favorites were Yossele Rosenblatt (whom Otis Spann might have appreciated), and the magisterial Moshe Koussevitzky, who sang in the last Yom Kippur service in Warsaw in 1939 before the Nazis turned the city into a charnel house.

For this set, Bernstein and the Sam Rivers trio hurl themselves into Bernstein's transcriptions of four of

Koussevitzky's recorded performances, his own response pieces, and two vintage Jewish songs.

I can hear the voice of the chazan in Bernstein's trumpet bringing me back to the first music that made me want to shout out loud in surprise at the emotions it released in me. In my memoir, *Boston Boy* (Paul Dry Books), I saw the chazan again in his black robes and high black skullcap.

"What he sings is partly written, largely improvised. He is a master of melisma—for each sacred syllable, there are three, four, six notes that climb and entwine, throbbing in wait for the next spiraling cluster. The chazan is a tenor, a dramatic tenor, in this continual dialogue with God . . . The cry. The *krechts* (a catch in the voice). A sob. A cry summoning centuries of hosts of Jews. The dynamics—a thunderstorm of fierce yearning that reverberates throughout the shul and then, as if the universe had lost a beat, there is a sudden silence, and from deep inside the chazan, a soaring falsetto. The room is swaying; his soul, riding a triumphant vibrato, goes right through the roof."

Such is the penetrating power on *Diaspora Blues* of Bernstein, Sam Rivers, Doug Mathews, and Anthony Cole. When I was about twelve, coming across black blues, I heard the *krechts*, the cry, there too, and again I felt like shouting aloud. And being outside the synagogue, I did.

On National Public Radio's *Fresh Air*, Kevin Whitehead said of Bernstein that "he has a focused, vocalized approach to trumpet, which is perfect for this project. Sometimes he also uses a plunger mute on the rare slide trumpet to sound even more voicelike."

Steven Bernstein and Sam Rivers—who hear music far beyond any stylistic boxes—share the passion to search for meaning in music and to find new dimensions of understanding themselves and the world.

In the October/November, 2002, issue of *The Absolute Sound*, reviewer Fred Kaplan says of *Diaspora Blues*: "Listening to their blues-drenched excursions into 'Aveinu Malkenu,' 'N'Kadesh Oz B'Kol,' and the Chanukah blessing, I couldn't help but reflect that if Sabbath services were like this, I'd go more often."

By and large, only in the Orthodox synagogues are the services any longer like the impressions on *Diaspora Blues*. Similarly, the root sound and rhythms in the Holiness churches that shaped the discovery of how liberating music can be for young black musicians years ago are also still resounding.

Diaspora Blues, a project of John Zorn's Tzadik label, is available at record stores, Amazon.com and Tzadik.com. For information on the history of the chazans, there is the newly published first paperback edition of *Chosen Voices: The Story of the American Cantorate* by Mark Slobin (University of Illinois Press).

The book is part of a long list of titles in the University's "Music in American Life" series. Among others are Mark Tucker's *Ellington: The Early Years* and *Hot Man: The Life of Art Hodes* by Hodes and Chadwick Hansen. Long ago, Hodes ran a jazz magazine, *The Jazz Record*, in which my first piece on the music appeared. So you could blame him, if he were still around, for what followed.

On the High Holidays, my father and I, after the services were over at our Orthodox synagogue, would walk around the neighborhood where there were other shuls. We would check out the chazans in each one—and rate them, annually. But I never could have imagined then that so many years later, I'd be hearing jazz chazans on *Diaspora Blues*.

At the end of *Chosen Voices*, Slobin says that what makes the American cantorate unique is "its intertwining, now inextricable, of strands of indigenous American popular forms." In *Diaspora Blues*, that multiculturalism works the other way too.

THE EVERLIVING BLUES

Jimmy Rushing was talking about the blues. "What they are," he said, "are he-she songs. So long as people have that feeling, that strong feeling, for each other, the blues are never going to die."

Remembering that conversation, I was startled to read this obituary by Peter Watrous in the June 27 *New York Times*: "The wells that gave rise to so much American music have seemingly dried up. Blues culture is dead." Just a month before, John Burnett was reporting on National Public Radio from the deepest source of historical black blues, the Mississippi Delta. But Burnett was not talking about the past. He was in the immediate present—telling how Johnnie Billington is teaching teenagers not only about the blues but how they can get inside the blues to tell their own stories.

Billington, a retired sixty-four-year-old auto mechanic and blues guitarist, has his own band—J.B. and the Midnighters—which has played at the Kennedy Center in Washington and, last August, at a blues festival in Norway. But his main gig these days is in schoolrooms and in Sarah's Kitchen, described by Burnett as "a narrow, smoky club in downtown Clarksdale, Mississippi."

There, fifteen-year-old Vanesia Young, one of Billington's students, is making the electric guitar conjugate the blues. Her mother, Katherine Young, tells Burnett: "At 5:00 in the morning, I'm laying in my bed, she's playing the blues on the piano. She gets up with the blues and goes to bed with the blues."

That's what Leadbelly used to say. The everliving blues culture is thriving not only in the Mississippi Delta, but in many recent blues recordings from Telarc, Delmark, Bullseye, Blind Pig, and Rounder. Not only the vintage blues bards are still telling stories, but younger enliveners of the tradition are also being heard.

Going back to Johnnie Billington's rounds, he stops at the Rosa Fort Middle School in Tunica, Mississippi. The teacher, twenty-four-year-old Robin Morris, has a degree in history and has been trying to get the kids involved in the rich blues history of where they actually live.

"It's exciting," she tells John Burnett, "to watch them catch onto it. They hated the blues music. They were saying, 'Oh, this is boring.' "

But then this nurturing teacher played Big Mama Thornton's "Hound Dog" and "they all jumped up and they were dancing around. Now they're all writing songs and the girls got together to write a song called, "All Men Are Hound Dogs." Like Jimmy Rushing said, the blues come down to he and she, and sometimes they come way down.

When Johnnie Billington is at the Rosa Fort Middle School, he puts together, from the beginning up, a blues band. And on National Public Radio, it played a slow blues in E Major. Johnnie, as everybody calls him, points to a youngster: "Yeah, see! He's feeling it see!" Katherine Young, the mother of Johnnie's fifteen-year-old student guitarist who's possessed by the blues, says: "You can feel that music more than any other music while you're playing it."

Years ago, when I was recording Otis Spann, one of the most penetrating of all blues singers and pianists, he told me how listeners feel the blues: "What they want from us are stories. The blues for them is something like a book. They want to hear stories out of their own experiences, and that's the kind we tell."

Young folks have plenty of experiences and once, as with Mr. Johnnie's students, the blues becomes their familiar language, it stays with them all their lives. At the Middle School in Tunica, John Burnett reports: "For the excited fifth-graders, fidgeting in their desks, a visit from Mr. Johnnie climaxes weeks of studying about the blues." Johnnie says to the kids: "Y'all got the blues and I know y'all are real young. What kind of blues you got? You got the blues for Kraft Macaroni & Cheese, right? But you see, what we sing is the things that you want. Blues is things that you want. Sometimes you don't have the money to get it right then."

Mr. Johnnie fixed up an old club, and high school students stop in on the way home from school. They not only work on the blues there. He counsels them too. What about? "Just about everything in life. How to carry yourself through the public. About life itself. Sex. That's the whole idea. The music I use is to get their attention." The blues, after all, is indeed about "life itself."

Consider all the culturally deprived American kids of all conceivable backgrounds who don't know about the blues. But there are many blues players who could tell them more about life itself if they were invited into the schools.

THE MASTERS

Jo Jones:
The Man Who Played
Like the Wind

Eddie Locke, a drummer who, on and off the stand, embodies the resilience of the jazz life, was an apprentice of Jo Jones. He carried Jones's drums to record dates, set them up and watched Jo's every move.

Locke spoke of Jo, and his own life in jazz, for the Hamilton College Jazz Archive, directed by Monk Rowe. The Archive's hundreds of oral histories range from Doc Cheatham to Bill Charlap.

"He was the most creative drummer I ever saw," Locke said of Jo. "He could create things I never saw anybody else do. And I'd never seen anybody play brushes the way he could. . . . The Basie rhythm section was just like the wind. It was so smooth."

One night, at Storyville in Boston, I saw Jo leave the stand and his drums, and with his hands as his only instrument, he moved around the room, playing with his fingers or the palms of his hands or his knuckles, conjuring up melodies, rhythms, cross-rhythms, from tables, chairs, walls, from the air itself.

As Eddie Locke said, Jo was a magician; everybody in the room, me included, was mesmerized as Jo, grinning fiercely, kept expanding and deepening jazz time, drawing us into his vortex for almost an hour.

Off the stand, Jo was just as unremittingly intense. To him jazz was religion. It was, he said, a God-given privilege to be able to play what you feel and to reach people because music, being the medium it is, can affect you all your life—the musician and the listener.

Jo was always on the lookout for beginners who, he felt, had the calling and needed his encouragement, instruction and, when necessary, his critique not only of their playing but of how they were living their lives. "There must be no debauchery attached to this music," he would say. It drained out the spirit of the music.

He occasionally included nonmusicians among his charges—his "kiddies," he called them. When I was nineteen, with a jazz program on Boston radio and spending most of my off hours at the Savoy Café, Jo Jones sat me down at a back table, and until closing told me where the music had come from, its soul force, and how to listen totally to what was inside the musicians, because that's what the music was all about. And, of course, I must avoid debauchery.

At Jo Jones' funeral on September 9, 1985, the front rows of St. Peter's Church in New York City were full of drummers. Max Roach stood up and told of how Jo would suddenly show up in the audience at a club where Max was playing—in Kansas City or Chicago—to check up on this "kiddie."

As I wrote in my report on that funeral in *Listen to the Stories*, Max recalled: "I played everything I could think of during that set. I hit everything I could hit. When the set was over, perspiring, I sat next to Jo and waited. He knew how much I wanted to know what he thought. Being Jo, he had to tell me what he had thought—straight. Finally, Jo said, 'All I could hear was your watch.' " There was a wave of laughter from the rows of jazz drummers.

I was thinking of Jo—his enveloping generosity of spirit, his devotion to the music that was his very life and his focus on the individual—during the discussion at the SFJAZZ Spring Season: "Is jazz black music?" (Part of that exchange was transcribed in the September 2001 issue of *JazzTimes*.) When I spoke, I made the obvious point that the roots of the music are black. But over time, though the primary originators—as contrasted with the originals, of whom there continue to be many—have been black, all the creators have become part of what Alan Lomax called "the rainbow of American music."

Jo Jones knew that back then. He didn't see the skin colors of his "kiddies." He listened to who they were, who they had been and where they were going.

Chip Stern was responsible for the most revealing interview Jo Jones ever gave. Jo told him: "I was born no child. I was born a man. Not a baby. Not a boy. A man in capital letters. No questions, no semicolons, no parentheses, no commas. Period. A man!"

A man whose music was universal.

Johnny Hodges:
Life Could Be a Dream
When He Blew Alto

At fourteen, I was waiting by the stage door of the RKO Theater in Boston, hoping to speak to Duke Ellington's legendary alto saxophonist, Johnny Hodges, between sets. I was going to say that like him, I grew up in Roxbury, a neighborhood of Boston, and like him, my first horn was the soprano saxophone. But when he came out the door, I was so in awe that I couldn't speak.

Recently, the international jazz impresario George Wein told a meeting of the Duke Ellington Society that, as a youngster, hearing Hodges "was a thrill equaled only by hearing Pavarotti and seeing Margot Fonteyn for the first time." And even Benny Goodman, exceedingly sparing of praise for anyone, said that Hodges was "by far the greatest man on alto that I ever heard."

Hodges did not take you by storm, as tenor saxophonist Coleman Hawkins did. While he was a virile swinger, Hodges's abiding impact was the sensuousness, the dreamlike eroticism, of his ballad playing. Duke Ellington told me that when the band played a dance, and Hodges soloed on "Warm Valley" or Billy Strayhorn's

"Passion Flower," inevitably a sigh would come from one of the dancers, and "that feeling," Duke said, "would become part of our music."

Back in Roxbury, alto saxophonist Charlie Holmes remembered hearing the thirteen-year-old Hodges, a neighbor. "I've never known anyone in my life just pick up an instrument and play it the way he did," Holmes told Ellington chronicler Stanley Dance. "I mean, he was playing it—he wasn't just playing with it. And without knowing anything about the keys, he'd just blow in any key. He was just a natural musician."

Imperturbable

No matter what he was playing, in any tempo, on the stand Hodges was imperturbable. "I've never been the emotional sort," he told the English jazz critic Max Jones. "I've never jumped around. I don't think a good showman is necessarily a good player."

At a dance in Boston in the late 1940s, I witnessed a test of Hodges's imperturbability. While Hodges was taking a solo, the dancers suddenly stopped, clearing a wide space for two angry men wielding knives, circling each other. The other Ellington musicians leaned forward, still playing but clearly fearful of the coming bloodshed. Hodges, looking on impassively, did not in the least break the romantic mood he was setting. The combatants were dragged off the floor, and the other musicians relaxed, but Hodges didn't have to.

Although aware of his importance to the Ellington orchestra—he felt he wasn't getting paid enough—Hodges preferred small combo settings. "You make a nice sound," he told Max Jones, "and that way you carry no passengers"—except the ones he selected.

Mosaic records—the Tiffany of jazz reissue labels—has recently released a box set, thoroughly annotated, of *The Complete Johnny Hodges Small Group Sessions 1956–61* (www.mosaicrecords.com, and in stores) for Verve. Verve was one of the late Norman Granz's labels. He recorded only the musicians he liked, often with little concern for sales prospects, but rather for posterity. During the years of these Hodges sessions, modern jazz (bebop) was ascendant, and Hodges, like many swing-era players, would not have been recorded nearly so often by any other producer.

There are ninety-five tracks. Among the various players are such Ellington colleagues as Lawrence Brown, Harry Carney, Ray Nance, and Billy Strayhorn. The formidable visitors include Roy Eldridge, Vic Dickenson, Ray Brown, Jimmy Rowles, and Jo Jones. On half of the numbers, tenor saxophonist Ben Webster, as vital to the Ellington sound as Hodges, is present. Webster could roar on up-tempos, but on ballads he was as masterfully intimate as the leader of these dates.

Bechet Plus Armstrong

Included are jubilant swingers, conversational blues, seamless duets, and other dimensions of jazz chamber music. Along with an abundance of standards, including Ellington's, there are rarer songs such as Strayhorn's "Ballad for Very Tired and Sad Lotus Eaters," "The Peaches Are Better Down the Road" (a blues for slow, close dancing) and the poignantly reflective "Just a Memory."

In the notes, Stanley Dance recalls Hodges saying of his years coming up in Roxbury that Sidney Bechet (who later became his mentor) and Louis Armstrong were his key influences: "I just put both of them together, and used a little of what I thought of new."

Baritone saxophonist Harry Carney, who became the anchor of the Ellington rhythm section for decades, was a neighbor of Hodges during their formative years and would often be at Hodges's home, where, as he told Mr. Dance, "being able to play some of the music on the records gave us the feeling of being sort of big-time musicians." Carney joined Ellington in 1927 and continued to play with the orchestra, eventually under Mercer Ellington's direction, until he died in 1974. Hodges became part of the band in 1928 and, except for relatively brief periods, sat in the reed section with Carney until he had a fatal heart attack in a dentist's chair in 1970.

Another newly released set of Johnny Hodges chamber music is *Things Ain't What They Used to Be: Johnny Hodges and Rex Stewart* (Koch Jazz), which he recorded in 1940 and 1941 with the longtime Ellington cornetist. On one of the dates—with Carney, Jimmy Blanton, Lawrence Brown, and other Ellington sidemen—Hodges plays Strayhorn's "Day Dream." It was one of his favorite songs. "When I'm playing that," he said, "it's supposed to be very, very soft, and you're supposed to close your eyes and dream awhile."

On the same session Hodges includes one of his own songs, "That's the Blues Old Man." It was his last recording on the soprano saxophone. As a kid, he was first attracted to that instrument "because it looked so pretty." Not even Bechet played it with such tenderness.

I later did get to talk to Johnny Hodges, and the only musician I've known who was more sparing of words was Benny Goodman. But Hodges didn't have to use words. "Music," he once said, "can soothe a lot of pain, and it'll get closer to people than money can."

CHARLES MINGUS:
MINGUS LIVES

Through the years, ghost bands have been roaming the nation bearing the names of dead leaders— Glenn Miller and Tommy Dorsey among them. The musicians play some of the repertory of the original orchestras and are fronted by surrogate leaders who play the instruments of the men after whom the bands are named. The sounds of the spectral travelers are familiar, but the spontaneity of the originals is missing.

There is, however, one such continuation of a leader's name that actually does keep alive his spirit and, in this case, his many voices. For six years, the Mingus Big Band has been playing at the Time Cafe's Fez room in lower Manhattan. Hearing it in person for the first time, it was as if the larger-than-life, volcanic Charles Mingus was there—shouting at his musicians to keep stretching themselves and never fake true improvisation.

I am not a believer in ghosts. But since Mingus was a friend for many years, I heard his groups more often than any others, and his presence is unmistakable through the empathy of the musicians in this band. He was one of the few jazzmen to create a considerable original body of work—among the others were Jelly Roll Morton, Duke Ellington, and Thelonious Monk. Mingus's compositions took many forms—as did he in the course of an evening. No one except Ellington could be more deeply, flowingly lyrical; but he could also explode with sardonic surprises. There were also meditations on death, the gracefulness of Lester Young, and the irrepressibility of Mingus's wife, Sue.

Sue Mingus, almost as indomitable a force as Charles, is responsible for creating and sustaining the Mingus Big Band. Charles often spoke to me of his dream of having a big band regularly rehearsing and playing his works, but he was never able to overcome the economics of that desire. Listening to this big band, Sue, who is at the Time Cafe every Thursday night, said, "If only Charles could be here!" And, for that matter, "If only Charles could see me now!"

There are at least 100 musicians available for gigs with the band, and they are among the best in New York. To cite a few: baritone saxophonist Ronnie Cuber, trumpeter Randy Brecker, Steve Slagle on alto and soprano saxophones, trombonist Robin Eubanks, and drummer Tommy Campbell, a wondrously attentive, flexible energizer of the band and each soloist.

Mingus's repertory was and is vast. A good many of his pieces have yet to be played by this band and some were never even performed in Mingus's time. Also, when he was afflicted with Lou Gehrig's disease and could no longer write, I remember him wordlessly singing new pieces into a tape recorder. Sue expects to have them scored.

The band has played Europe six times and tours in the U.S. It has been filmed by Japanese, Italian, and German television, and makes recordings on the Dreyfus label (212-818-0770). One of the sets is *Live in Time*, recorded, as the title indicates, at the Time Cafe, with Sue Mingus as producer.

Mingus was not in the least reticent in complaining about injustices. He wrote fierce letters to jazz magazines in answer to critics he felt ought to have gone into another line of work. And he was furious about record piracy. Two of his 1964 Paris concerts, for example, were pirated, and he keep brooding that his musicians had not been paid.

In later years, Sue Mingus took up that fight. One day she scooped up a number of pirated Mingus sets in a Paris record store and would not pay for them. She challenged the staff to have her arrested for taking property that had been stolen from her husband. On her own Revenge label, moreover, she issued recordings of those two Paris concerts, undercutting the pirates by charging a lower price. And, at last, the musicians on the CD were paid—by Sue. She has also sent lists of pirated records and CDs to record stores throughout the country, and now the pirates are being exposed on the Mingus Web site (www.mingus-mingusmingus.com).

Mingus was fifty-six when he died in 1979. In addition to his composing and direction of various groups, he was the most accomplished—and astonishing—bassist in jazz history. As for his personality, while he was capable of being gentle and generous, he could—as Sue admits—be intimidating at times. And he was never predictable. He would even change shape, losing large amounts of weight and later putting it all back again. And like Duke Ellington, in his disdain for stereotypes, he had no patience with those who limited music by putting it into categories.

As a sideman, Mingus worked with Louis Armstrong, Kid Ory, Red Norvo, Charlie Parker, Duke Ellington, Bud Powell, and Art Tatum. The time with Tatum brought Mingus great satisfaction because, years before, he had tried to sit in with Tatum, who had laughed at his presumptuousness.

In a club, and sometimes during a concert, Mingus would stop the music and berate one or more members of the group for slipping into familiar licks. Sitting at the Time Cafe, suddenly shouting with the joy of the music—as I sometimes had when he was in charge—I doubted that Mingus would have commanded this big band to halt so he could reprimand it. Instead, he might have started writing for it all night long.

Mingus best defined himself. "I'm trying," he told me, "to play the truth of what I am. The reason it's difficult is because I'm changing all the time."

Now his scores, manuscripts, and tapes of him composing at the piano are in the Library of Congress. But the Mingus musicians, as he instructed all his players, keep searching for themselves in his music, creating new inner shapes and dynamics, so that even posthumously, Mingus keeps changing.

CHARLES MINGUS:
THE INCOMPLETE HISTORY
OF CHARLES MINGUS

The most widely read book review section in the country is in the Sunday *New York Times*; and on August 6, 2000, Gene Santoro's biography of Charles Mingus, *Myself When I Am Real* (Oxford University Press), was reviewed by Daniel Mark Epstein. More people will now think they know who Mingus was than the total readers combined of Santoro's work and the other books about Mingus.

Epstein has written a useful biography of Nat King Cole (Farrar Straus & Giroux), but what he says he has learned from Santoro's book is that "Mingus was selfish and mean and violent. . . . What made Mingus great was his discipline and maturity as a musician. His refusal to grow up made him nothing but newspaper copy, a sideshow and a heartache to everyone who loved him."

Nothing in the review reveals what was "great" about Mingus' music, and the still uninformed reader would have no idea why Gunther Schuller has said: "Mingus' music is one of the widest ranging musics you can find, composed by one single human being. It covered the entire range of human emotions. So, he reflected exactly who he was in his music." Schuller said that in the course of Don McGlynn's film *Charles Mingus: Triumph of the Underdog* (co-produced by Sue Mingus), which goes deeper into the indivisible life and music of Mingus than any writing about him so far.

As for Mingus the "sideshow" and "heartache to everyone who loved him," I knew Charles from the time we were both in our twenties, first in Boston when he came there as a sideman. When he was on the road, we corresponded, and after I went to New York in 1953 to write for *Down Beat*, our lives, professional and personal, continually intersected.

One of the last times I saw him, trying to conquer Lou Gehrig's disease, he could not move except to hum into a tape recorder a new composition that the remarkably attuned Sy Johnson would later orchestrate for a record date.

As a reporter and friend, I have known all kinds of people, from Supreme Court Justice William Brennan to John Cardinal O'Connor and Bayard Rustin, longtime strategist for Dr. Martin Luther King. I have never known anyone as nakedly honest as Mingus and as knowledgeable of the way the world works and as hopeful of how it should work if there were indeed "equal justice under the laws," as the Constitution tries to guarantee.

Yes, Mingus was volcanic and sometimes exploded, but he was the closest, most stimulating and reliable friend I've ever had. In his *New York Times* review, Daniel Mark Epstein says with certainty that Mingus "blamed his troubles on racism." Mingus was hardly passive whenever Jim Crow came around the corner, but it was Mingus who told me: "It's not only a question of color anymore. It's getting deeper than that, I mean it's getting more and more difficult for a man or woman just to love. People are getting so fragmented, and part of that is that fewer and fewer people are making a real effort anymore to find out exactly who they are. Most people are forced to do things they don't want to most of the time, and so they get to the point where they no longer have any choice about anything important, including who they are. We create our own slavery. But I'm going to keep getting through and finding out the kind of man I am through my music."

Epstein, I expect, can't be blamed for the headline of his *New York Times* review, "The Big Bebopper," but seeing that would have instantly impelled Mingus to send a stinging letter to the editor of the *New York Times Book Review*.

This was "the big bebopper" who—when he was still unknown and playing in Kid Ory's band on the West Coast—was told by Fats Navarro: "That's not it, Mingus, that's what they used to do."

"Well," Mingus recalled, "I'm not going to worry about that sort of thing anymore. I said to myself at the time. I'm going to be me. And nowadays, if Bird himself were to come back to life, I wouldn't do something just because he did it. I'd have to feel it, too."

Santoro's book was reviewed in the August 22, 2000, *Wall Street Journal* by Phil Pastras. What he thought of its deficiencies is indicated by Pastras' first sentence: "Someday, someone will tell Charles Mingus' story as it deserves to be told, will capture his gargantuan passions and appetites and show how they relate in some way to a body of work that expresses in music the fullness of the American experiences."

Maybe no one book can do it, but there will soon be a memoir by Sue Mingus who has kept Charles' music—and therefore the meaning of his life—alive through the Mingus bands and orchestras she keeps in motion. The depth of the man and his music is such that these musicians never tire of investigating Mingus—or his creations.

LESTER YOUNG:
HE ALWAYS TOLD A STORY

In what may be one of the more original and illuminating ideas in the history of jazz recording, Verve has
started an "Ultimate" series in which contemporary
musicians of note select recordings by vintage players and
comment on how they were influenced by their elders.
Among the sets are Roy Hargrove on Dizzy Gillespie,
James Carter on Ben Webster, and Nicholas Payton on
Clifford Brown.

Included in Verve's reservoir of historic recordings are
many of Norman Granz's releases. Granz, an ardent and
brusque jazz fan and entrepreneur, would only record
artists he admired, and he kept them on his label even if
sales of their recordings were considerably less than abun-
dant. Once, when a marketing man complained that
pianist Tommy Flanagan had sold only 1,500 copies over
some time, Granz angrily told him, "If 1,500 people want
to hear Tommy Flanagan, they should be able to!"

One of Granz's favorites was Lester Young, who—in
my view—was the most continually and subtly creative
tenor saxophonist in jazz. In Verve's *Ultimate Lester*

Young, the guide to his style and influence is Wayne Shorter, who, like hundreds of other tenors, was shaped in part by Lester.

Among the eleven tracks, recorded between 1946 and 1956, are sessions with pianist Nat "King" Cole, who also knew the difference between mere technical virtuosity and the essential art in jazz of—as Lester put it—"telling a story."

There is also a selection—"I Didn't Know What Time It Was"—from a 1956 date that I would rate as one of the most indispensable jazz sets ever recorded. Titled *The Jazz Giants* and produced by Granz, it includes trumpeter Roy Eldridge; trombonist Vic Dickenson (who also knew how to use the space between notes); pianist Teddy Wilson; and Count Basie drummer Jo Jones, known back then as "the man who played like the wind."

Wayne Shorter also picked a classic definition of exhilarating collective swinging—the kind of groove, as Jo Jones used to say, that made you walk out of a jazz club in tempo. The tune is "Lester Leaps In," and among his colleagues are fellow Basie alumni: trumpet player Buck Clayton, trombonist Dicky Wells, Jo Jones, and guitarist Freddie Green, who rightly regarded himself as the master of "the rhythm wave."

On three of the other tracks, Lester improvises with the warmly compatible trumpet player Harry "Sweets" Edison. Once, at a rehearsal for a tribute to his employer, Count Basie, I saw Edison frown at an arrangement that had just been brought in by a skillful but rather too technically proficient writer.

Sweets stopped the music. "Too many notes," he said, and crossed out a bunch of them from his part. He also slowed down the tempo so the music—and the musicians—could breathe. Lester came from the same school: Less is much more to the point when you're telling a story.

In his notes to his Lester Young lesson plan, Wayne Shorter says: "You know how the usual tenor saxophonist will run up and down? Pres doesn't do that. Pres gets closer to what music is for. . . . Pres expresses how he *feels*."

John Lewis, musical director of the Modern Jazz Quartet, recognized that way back when. "The basic mark of Lester"—Mr. Lewis told me during the period of these recordings—"is that he's always young. He stays young in his playing and in his person. Some people are always crying for love and kindness; but Lester doesn't cry. The way he seems to see *being* is: 'Here we are. Let's have a nice time.' "

Even in his last years of physical decline, before his early death at age forty-nine in 1959, Pres remained gentle, kind, and extraordinarily considerate of other people's feelings, living up to the fond title bestowed on him by Billie Holiday as the president of the tenor saxophone.

Off the stand as well as on the job, Lester was immediately distinctive in appearance. Mr. Shorter recalls his porkpie hat (Charles Mingus wrote a threnody for Pres, "Goodbye, Porkpie Hat") and his customary "long [black] coat with the raglan sleeves." Lester sort of floated when he walked. And when he played, he once said of himself, "I'm always loose in space, lying out there somewhere."

Like Duke Ellington, Lester didn't like to dwell on the past, on his past recordings. In a 1959 interview with the French critic François Positif, he said: "I developed my tenor to sound like an alto, to sound like a tenor, to sound like a bass, and I'm not through with it all yet. That's why they [the critics] get all trapped up. They say, 'Goddamn, I never heard Pres play like this!' That's the way I want them to hear. That's *modern*, you dig?"

If Lester Young had been asked to participate in an "Ultimate Series," I expect he would have chosen recordings by Frankie Trumbauer, who played the C-melody saxophone with Bix Beiderbecke.

"When I had just started to play," Pres told me one afternoon, "Trumbauer was my idol. I used to buy all his records. I imagine I can still play all those solos off the record. I tried to get the sound of a C-melody on a tenor. That's why I don't sound like other people. And I liked the way he slurred the notes. He'd play the melody first and then after that, he'd play around the melody."

Jimmy Rushing, Count Basie's nonpareil singer, said of Pres: "He was always different. If he'd follow a guy's solo, you'd think he'd go one way, but he'd always go the other. He could play an odd note, and you'd think, 'Gee, he'd better leave it alone because now it's going to be all wrong if he goes on with it.' But it wasn't. He'd always have another note next to that one to slip into. He played on a note like you would play on a word."

DUKE ELLINGTON:
DUKE ELLINGTON'S MISSION

The world-renowned Duke Ellington and his orchestra were on their usual round of one nighters. On Route 66 in Illinois, less than 100 miles south of Chicago, "we stopped at a gas station," Duke reminisced, "and there was a little coffee shop. I walked in and said, 'I'd like to have a stick of gum.' I mean a package of chewing gum. And this very nice girl came to me and said, like she was reading it, 'I'm sorry, sir, but I cannot serve you.'" Duke, the grandson of slaves, paused in the telling. "She couldn't serve me a stick of chewing gum!"

During the height of the civil rights movement, Ellington was hurt and angry at the charge by some activists that he considered himself above the battle—that he had not spoken out boldly enough against racism. "People who think that of me," Duke told me then, 'have not been listening to our music. For a long time, social protest and the pride in the Negro [an acceptable word at that time] have been the most significant things in what we've done. In that music we have been telling for a long time what it is to be a Negro in this country."

He also told me of how, in the 1920s, he had said to Fletcher Henderson, "Why don't we drop the word, 'jazz,' and call what we're doing, 'Negro music.' Then there won't be any confusion." It was too bold an idea for Fletcher Henderson.

Ellington was not a chauvinist. He was a multi-culturalist before the word was ever current ("The Far East Suite," "The Afro-Eurasian Eclipse," et al.). But he did "seriously believe," he once told a radio interviewer, "that the Negro has more to offer emotionally than any other single group in this country. His emotions—by the very necessity of the circumstances—form an integral part of America. By that I do not mean that our race is sad and depressed, nor happy and hilarious. But we have tasted both extremes of this range, and we have learned to accomplish the transition from the depths to the heights with greater authority than the average human."

In 1943, I heard, for the first time, "Black, Brown and Beige"—Ellington's personal illumination of the range of the black experience in America. It was at Symphony Hall in Boston, and corny as this sounds, it changed my life. It made me begin to see, feel, and understand the deepest and most abiding failure of this constitutional democracy.

The work started, as Duke once described it, "in the hold of the slave ship where it's black in every way you can think of. In America, they found out they were only going to work. And along came the work songs, the spirituals." There is so much more of indelible black history in that composition, and in so many others by Ellington. There are tributes ("Black Beauty"); richly vivid details of black life ("Harlem Suite," "Harlem Airshaft"); the price of survival ("The Deep South Suite"); and scores more original and universal expressions of the black American experience.

"I always had my mind," Duke said, "on the teacher I had in the eighth grade. A lady by the name of Mrs. Boston. She was the principal, and she used to teach race pride as much as she did English. She said, When you go out, represent respect—and demand respect.

In the years before the civil rights movement, Ellington emphasized, "we did not play before segregated audiences. And, when we first went down South, we would charter two Pullman cars and park in the station. We didn't have a hotel problem. It was as if the president was on tour. We commanded respect."

As for Ellington's musical mission, Albert Murray gets to the core of his triumph: "I don't think anybody has achieved a higher synthesis of the American experience than Duke Ellington. Anybody who achieved a literary equivalent of that would be beyond Melville, Henry James, and Faulkner. He transformed the experience of American Negroes . . . in the actual texture of all human existence, not only in the United States but in all places throughout the ages."

His music should be played in schools throughout the nation—starting in the elementary grades. He should be a presence in courses in American history. Not only in black history courses, but in all American studies. In Albert Murray's term, Duke was an omni-American.

Duke Ellington died on May 24, 1974. The month before, I was one of a number of people who received a Christmas card from his hospital room. He was always looking ahead.

DUKE ELLINGTON:
THE PIANO PLAYER IN THE BAND

As a teenager in Boston, I faithfully went to Ellington dance dates as well as his Symphony Hall concerts. Not to dance. I've never learned. I came to hear what is usually regarded as his primary instrument, his nonpareil orchestra, composed of what were even then legendary soloists—Johnny Hodges, Cootie Williams, Rex Stewart, Ben Webster, "Tricky Sam" Nanton, and so on.

But I would make sure to arrive early to hear an unannounced set of solo piano. Some of the stars in the band competed as to who could make the latest entrance, thereby signifying his ultimate importance. Ellington, not much of a disciplinarian, would wait at the piano, improvising for himself what often later turned out to be new compositions.

He didn't need a rhythm section, since he lived in jazz time. Ellington delighted in exploring and extending all the resources of the piano, having been much impressed when he came to New York in the early 1920s by several masters of stride piano—a discipline with roots in ragtime that required the continuous use of both hands and the energy to keep rent parties roaring. But his piano mentors—Willie "The Lion" Smith, Luckey Roberts, and James P. Johnson—were also melodists with a lyrical grace who could keep the surrounding conversation low.

A Distinctive Touch

As Ralph Gleason writes in the notes to *Duke Ellington: The Pianist* (Fantasy), Ellington soon developed "a personal sound on the piano. Let Duke strike a chord and you knew it was Duke and no one else." In this Fantasy set, Ellington—with a rhythm section—ranges from a sensuous "Slow Blues" made for very intimate dancing to a gently elegant threnody for his longtime collaborator, Billy Strayhorn, "Never Stop Remembering Bill."

The session exemplifies Mr. Gleason's wonder at Ellington's ability to switch moods from "the suave, international boulevardier" to "the raunchiest backroom, after hours piano player." For instance, his "Sam Woodward's Blues" had me shouting aloud as if I were in a back room with an open bar near dawn.

In a recent *JazzTimes* magazine tribute to the piano player in the band, Fred Hersch, himself an original jazz pianist, speaks of Ellington's completely "distinctive touch" and says, "Like Thelonious Monk [who was also shaped by stride pianists], he had a way of creating musical space around the notes so that they had musical weight. . . . Though his touch was different from Count Basie's, his solos and comping also had a way of saying a lot with a little. A completely underrated pianist."

During an evening of reminiscing by Ellington alumni at New York's Jazz at Lincoln Center habitat in January, singer Milt Grayson focused on Ellington the accompanist: "He was the greatest accompanist in the world. You could stand up there and you didn't have to worry about anything. Duke Ellington was with you. And he just called himself 'the piano player.' "

Live at the Whitney

The instrumentalists felt the same way, and I would recommend listening to the orchestra recordings with particular attention to how the piano player lifted both the soloists and the ensemble sections—often with an accompanying shout of pride in his unerring taste in selecting "these expensive gentlemen," as he called his traveling companions.

Ellington seldom recorded without the orchestra, but another unveiling of the man at the piano is *Duke Ellington Live at the Whitney* (Impulse/GRP Records). The recital took place at the New York museum in April 1972, and it included what he was able to remember of "the first thing I ever played," the hurtling "Soda Fountain Rag." There is also a long dramatic section from Ellington's "New World A-Coming," a civil-rights anthem without polemics; and a tribute to "The Night Shepherd," New York pastor John Gensel, who ministered, full-time, to jazz people. Like Ellington, the pastor was an excellent listener and therefore knew how to time his counseling.

Ellington introduces each number in his playful way. He liked to put people on, softly. Once, standing at the entrance to a club, I saw the band playing, but the piano chair was empty. Suddenly, I felt a hand on my shoulder and heard a familiar voice behind me saying with regal diction, "You don't know who I am, but I know who you are."

Strayhorn Duets

As his sidemen used to tell me, it was often impossible when the band confronted a new composition to tell which part was Ellington and which was Strayhorn, so close was their collaboration. That deep mutual accord is impressively evident in *Great Times! Duke Ellington Billy Strayhorn Piano Duets* (Riverside/Fantasy). They often played together at parties, and Ellington's son, Mercer, along with jazz critic Leonard Feather, set up this recording session in 1950. There were no arrangements; having been so mutually attentive to each other for so long, they didn't need any charts. They just sat down and let the music take shape. Later, Strayhorn said about listening to the recordings, "I really have to sit down at a keyboard and play it out myself to know for sure who is playing."

Along with the somber and reflective "In Blue Summer Garden," the two dive into a powerful down-home "Bang-Up Blues" and a deeply felt memorial, "Blues for Jimmy Blanton," the Ellington bassist from whom all subsequent jazz bassists flowed.

Throughout this centennial year of Ellington's birth, there will be many concerts and radio series celebrating his other instrument, the orchestra; but these recordings are an invigorating reminder that the man at the piano could be an orchestra unto himself.

DUKE ELLINGTON:
INSIDE THE ELLINGTON BAND

No organization anywhere in the world has devoted as much space and care in illuminating the Duke Ellington Centennial as Jazz at Lincoln Center: Continuous concerts of his music across this country and others, panel discussions, and an Essentially Ellington High School Band Competition.

For me, exhilarated by Ellington since I was eleven years old, the most intriguing recent session was "Happy Reunion: Memories of Duke," during which alumni of the band spoke of what it was like to be part of that orchestra far beyond category. Listening, I remembered what Duke told me once when I asked him what his criterion was for enlisting a new sideman. "First of all," he said, "I want someone who knows how to listen." I never fully realized what he meant until I heard the alumni.

For instance, bassist Jimmy Woode told that night of being faced with "a piece of manuscript of four to five pages. You'd have maybe these forty-seven bars with notes, and then there'd be nothing for another twenty bars. When you'd ask, he'd say, 'Well, you know what not to do.' " Trombonist Buster Cooper: "I first joined the band in a recording studio. He was writing and said: 'Buster, I want you to take eight choruses on this tune.' I said, "Fine, but where's the chord changes?' Duke said, 'Chord changes? Listen, sweetie!' "

Once, explaining to me how he wrote for the band, Duke emphasized that he wrote for each musician. "I know their strengths," he said, "and their weaknesses." Trombonist John Sanders (now a monsignor in the Catholic Church): "The copyist not only had to copy the notes from the scores to the individual parts, but you didn't copy 'first trumpet,' 'third trombone' or 'fourth tenor sax.' You copied parts named for Johnny, for Harold, for Russell, for Brit, for Butter, for Ray Nance." Duke wanted musicians who had their own stories to tell. Trombonist Britt Woodman told of how much he admired Lawrence Brown and when he first joined the band, Britt played on "Sophisticated Lady" some of the licks that Lawrence Brown used to play. He was called into the maestro's dressing room. "Britt," said Duke, "I'm very sorry I called that number. Whenever you play, I want you to play yourself."

Duke was not much of a disciplinarian, but even he had limits of tolerance. Al Hibbler wanted very much to sing with the band and one night, after sitting in, he was told by Duke, "Pack your bags and meet me at the train at 4 o'clock tomorrow." Hibbler celebrated by getting plastered, and at the train station, he staggered up to Duke, who said, "You're not ready." Ivie Anderson tried to intercede. "Governor," she said to Duke, "keep him, and I'll straighten him out." "Look, Ivie," Duke said, "I can handle a blind man, but a blind drunk, I cannot." Trombonist Vince Prudente, who was with Duke the last two years of the band, noted that Duke didn't have to fire anyone who wasn't making it musically: "How can you be playing and see him over there and not try your best? I think if you didn't pretty soon you just left on your own because you realized the water was a little too deep for you." Tenor saxophonist Harold Ashby told of a call he got from Ben Webster just after Ashby had joined the band: "Vibe the Governor and Rab [Duke and Johnny Hodges] a little smile from me. Now you'll get your PhD in music, because you're with the Boss."

Drummer Butch Ballard summed up what I'd heard through the years from other alumni about the experience night after night of being in the middle of Duke's creation: "When Ray Nance (we called him Nancy) got up to play a solo, you knew it was Nancy. And he played it with such beauty and such warmth along with Mex (Paul Gonsalves), you had to just sit up there and just feel good all over your body when you heard these guys play. You don't hear that no more. You don't hear that kind of beauty when a guy plays a ballad no more. Like when Johnny Hodges would walk out front."

But you couldn't let yourself get lost in all that beauty and warmth. Bassist Arron Bell: "You had to keep your ears cocked and your eyes open. You would ask Duke, 'What chord is that?,' and he'd say, 'Huh?' He never would answer you. He always wanted you to go for yourself." But coming into the band was like entering Camelot. Vocalist Dolores Morgan Parker: "I was singing, and

Johnny Hodges came and stood beside me. I looked and said, 'My God, I'm standing next to Johnny Hodges!' "

When I was a kid, I once went up to Johnny Hodges at the stage door of a theater. I started to speak and couldn't. I too was struck with awe.

PHIL WOODS:
THE IRREPRESSIBLE SPIRIT OF JAZZ

Whenever I hear Phil Woods, he reminds me of Roy Eldridge. It's the passion of his story-telling and, like Roy, he never coasts. Eldridge, in rehearsals or on a gig, played as if it was the last chorus he'd ever take. So too with Phil Woods.

Yet, as Richard Cook and Brian Morton say in *The Penguin Guide to Jazz on CD*, Phil "has often suffered from a degree of neglect." When Phil was coming up, it was said by some that he was just an acolyte of Charlie Parker. But he soon came into his own compelling, resounding voice. And always, as Cook and Morton note, "he has a bottomless appetite for playing." It's long past time for a television profile of Phil, who has never stopped surprising himself.

Phil was one of the players on Dizzy Gillespie's 1956 State Department tour of Latin America and the Middle East. At twenty-three, Quincy Jones was chosen to be musical director and arranger for the band, and he put it together.

Dave Usher's three-volume set, *Dizzy in South America: Official State Department Tour 1956* (Red Anchor) is an exultant reminder of how much excitement and sheer pleasure we've lost as big league jazz bands vanished. The third CD includes Usher's interviews with Dizzy, Quincy and, among the sidemen, Phil Woods.

"Dizzy," says Phil, "is pivotal to the whole core of my being. He used to say, 'I'm a rhythm man. The rhythm is the foundation of the building. If you lose sight of the foundation, the building topples.'" And, Phil went on, "if you lose the basic spirit of the rhythm, when you get way out with harmonies and other things, you lose the jazz pulse. It's not jazz."

I thought of that reminder when I saw the lead paragraph on a *New York Times* piece, "Techno Dances With Jazz": "Wielding samplers and laptops instead of saxophones and pianos, electronic musicians are increasingly borrowing from—and aspiring to make—jazz." I can imagine Ben Webster's reaction to having a laptop in his rhythm section.

Phil was not saying that jazz, to be "authentic," has to be closed to other cultures and times. "Dizzy," Phil said in the interview, "was a student of music all his life. On his night off in another country, he'd say, 'I don't want to hear a jazz band. I want to hear their music.'" But Dizzy never lost sight of the jazz pulse. Nor did Duke Ellington, who absorbed colors and cadences, from every country he toured.

Phil also pointed out the influences on jazz of what he called "the Jewish-European harmonic contribution. Jerome Kern, Irving Berlin, and the rest of those composers fed the bebop soul. They weren't all Jewish. Cole

Porter, for example. And Dizzy collated all that. Along with the rhythm, Birks absorbed and expanded the harmonic sophistication of that tradition. With him, you got the whole package."

As direct and unguarded off the stand as he is when he speaks through his alto saxophone, Phil told a rite-of-passage story during the interview with Usher: "One night, at a club, I was down. I was saying, 'I'm not going anywhere, I'm a white guy in this music.' Hearing me whining and crying the blues, Art Blakey and Dizzy kidnapped me. They put me in a cab and took me to Dizzy's place in Long Island. Dizzy sat me down and said to me: 'Bird gave it to everybody. To all races. If you can hear it, you can play it.'"

What Phil misses these nights—and Quincy Jones has said this to me too—is what he calls "the oral tradition of the tribe. On the band bus, the young guys and the old guys would be together, and that's how we young guys learned. But there aren't any of those kinds of buses any more. There was a sharing thing, a family thing."

But the life force of the music goes on; and during the interview, Phil, putting into words what you hear on his horn, practically shouted: "I'm so lucky to be a jazz musician!"

It is, of course, undeniable that, as Sidney Bechet used to say, you can't hold the music back. Among the younger veterans, Dave Douglas doesn't hold back, nor does Greg Osby, to name a few. But as Ruby Braff knows, shows, and says: "Jazz is not exclusively a young man's music. It's in the first twenty-five years that you learn how to play your horn."

And Ben Webster once told me: "It may be that the older some players get, the better they are. At least I hope so. You keep hearing different guys and learning different things, and that helps."

Duke Ellington, when I asked him what he most looked for in bringing a new player into the band, did not mention age. "The most important thing is listening. That's the first important step in becoming a musician. If and when they stop listening—to themselves or to somebody else—they're no longer with music."

That also applies to those who don't play, but listen. Not by style or age, but to the life story of each member of the tribe.

Frankie Newton:
The Search for Frankie Newton

O n May 31, 2002, in conjunction with the second annual Highlands Jazz Festival in Abingdon, Virginia, the Historical Society of Washington County sponsored a program on "the life and music of Frankie Newton, legendary jazz artist and Washington County native." I doubt if many residents of Washington County had ever heard of Frankie Newton. For that matter, I wonder how many readers of *JazzTimes* know much if anything about a trumpet player whose first recording was on Bessie Smith's "Gimme a Pigfoot," and later accompanied Billie Holiday on "Strange Fruit." Admired by both Louis Armstrong and Dizzy Gillespie, Frankie, who was a friend of mine, was matched only by Miles Davis for intimately evocative and lyrical storytelling.

There are a number of musicians who, in their time, contributed uniquely to jazz history. But except for glancing references in books on jazz, they are largely unknown to relatively new listeners and are often hazily remembered by veteran enthusiasts. For example, when was the last time you heard about Emmett Berry, Irving Fazola, Lou McGarity, Gus Johnson, Pete Brown, or Brad Gowans?

When Frankie Newton died, at age forty-eight, in 1954, I wrote in *Down Beat* of his work with Cecil Scott, Elmer Snowden, Teddy Hill, and his own combos, one of which became the John Kirby band. "He is remembered," I added, "with special affection by the scores of children he helped introduce to music over the years during summers as a counselor in camps for underprivileged kids."

I'd come to know Frankie Newton in Boston where he often played, and later in New York, as a man of stubborn integrity (on and off the stand), a political dissenter, and an omnivorous reader, who would counsel friends to read James Joyce. In the obituary I wrote, I told of a friend of his, to whom Frankie was teaching trumpet. He insisted on paying for the lesson, and Frankie said: "Well, how much should I charge you per note? Look, if someone wants to learn how to play an instrument, if he loves music that much, there should be some way he can learn, whether he has the money to pay for it or not."

So how did Frankie Newton come to be on a jazz festival program about his life, as well as in a monograph, "The Search for Frankie Newton," published this year by the Historical Society of Washington County, Virginia—a study that led to his being part of the Highlands Jazz Festival? A couple of years ago, a woman from that county, Jennifer Wagner, who is white, called me. Then president of the historical society, she had seen a reference to the fact that this black jazz trumpet player had been born and grew up near her, and she wanted to find out more about him. She interviewed me over time, and I gave her leads to Roy Haynes, George Wein, and other sources.

It took her a lot of time and digging because there aren't that many writings about Newton, but she persevered and became increasingly intrigued with this fiercely independent, generous musician who, as she quotes from the July 1946 issue of *The Jazz Record*, "went his own way and did as he pleased. He consistently stayed out of big bands (after a while), lived his own life, preferred to scuffle with his own little group and do recording dates rather than tie himself to any schedule." Wagner mentions a January 13, 1939, Bluebird recording by Frankie, "The Blues My Baby Gave to Me," that I nearly wore out as a teenager. Now that RCA Victor has imaginatively regenerated the Bluebird archives, I hope that this deeply personal, and yet universal, classic illumination of jazz lovemaking will be available again. Maybe a consortium of labels for which Frankie recorded can compile a definitive Frankie Newton collection.

Wagner's monograph begins with Frankie Newton's birth—"in Blacksburg, a small settlement of African-Americans near Emory, Virginia. At the time of his childhood, the state of Virginia provided a segregated education through seventh grade or up to the age of fourteen." She adds, "It seems unlikely that he had ever heard jazz being played before leaving Washington County."

I also hope that others for whom jazz has become part of their life force will research and write about other musicians who have been long overlooked in the history of this indispensable music.

In Boston I spent most of my time, away from work, at the Savoy Café, where Frankie often played. I was not so much dating, as hoping to date, a singer on a gig there, and sometimes I walked her home in the black section of Boston. A black police detective, an equal-opportunity bruiser of suspects he collared, also had eyes for her, and resented my attentions to the singer. Frankie Newton, tall and athletic (he loved playing tennis), took to walking behind us when I walked the singer home after the last set at the Savoy. He knew of the black cop's explosiveness. I appreciated his riding shotgun for us, but all Frankie would say was, "Well, you're not hiding."

Wagner quotes Dan Morgenstern when Frankie died: "He was no ordinary man, and the music he made was no ordinary music. He was a poet; his recorded solos have a poignant lyricism of their own."

CECIL TAYLOR:
IT'S ABOUT MUSIC
AND CAPTURING SPIRITS

I've known Cecil Taylor since he was nineteen and I was twenty-seven. We met at a record store that was built into a side of Symphony Hall in Boston. He was studying at the New England Conservatory of Music. We'd go to classical music concerts—all of music was of intense interest to him. Then, as since, he had definite, contrarian, fierce opinions.

Early on, in jazz, he had been drawn to what he called "the beacons—lights indicating a certain direction." He cited Ellington, Lunceford, Chick Webb, Fats Waller—"A giant piano player. He could push a group no end. When he played the piano, it sang."

But when Cecil tried to become part of the New York jazz scene, many renowned musicians didn't hear any melody or sense. At one session, when Cecil sat in, Jo Jones exploded in revulsion and threw his top cymbal across the room. When Cecil got a Monday night gig at Birdland, Miles Davis, in the audience, listened, cursed, and walked out.

There was a period when gigs were so scarce that Cecil survived by working as a cook, dishwasher, deliveryman for a coffee shop, and record salesman. I saw him on the street one day, and he said he hadn't played before an audience in six months. But every night in his room, he told me, he played a full, imaginary concert before an audience in his head.

"I have to make that imaginative leap," he said. "I have to believe I'm communicating to somebody. I have to keep the contact going."

But when he found actual audiences, he sometimes electrified them. I first became aware of the impact my thorny friend could have at the Great South Bay Festival in 1958. At the center of the event was a reunion of the Fletcher Henderson band, and many of what were then called traditionalists were in the audience.

Whitney Balliett described what happened when Cecil came on: "[Part of the audience] fidgeted, whispered and wandered nervously in and out of the tent, as if the ground beneath had suddenly become unbearably hot."

But there were also listeners who first appeared mesmerized, and when the set was over, they ran, as if on fire, to reach Cecil and find out where they could buy his recordings.

Years later, toward the end of his presidency, Jimmy Carter held a jazz festival on a lawn of the White House. It wasn't one of those "star" performances at a state dinner, or the kind of honors ceremony at which Richard Nixon had the chutzpah to play a two-piano duet with the ever-gracious Duke Ellington.

Carter was a jazz fan. In his introduction, he told of how he had, before becoming an eminence, frequented jazz clubs, and he said something no other president had said before: jazz did not have the stature it deserved in its native land because of the racism here.

George Wein had orchestrated an intriguing sequence of performers—from Eubie Blake to Max Roach and Dizzy Gillespie. At the end, Dizzy cajoled the president to sing the "Salt Peanuts" refrain as he and Max accompanied the chief executive on that bop anthem.

A number of cabinet members were in the front seats throughout the concert. One of them was Attorney General Griffin Bell, in private life a powerful Atlanta attorney, who for years since has been a partner in one of the most successful law firms in the country, and a sometime presidential adviser.

When Cecil started his set, Jimmy Carter leaned forward, immobile, fixing his attention on the kinetic pianist. When Cecil hit the last thunderous notes, he made one of his high-speed exits, rushing into the shrubbery. The president leapt off his seat and chased Cecil until he cornered him.

Later, I asked Cecil, "What the hell did he want?"

"He wanted," Cecil said matter-of-factly, "to know where he could get some of my records."

Throughout his life in jazz, Cecil continues to spellbind or infuriate listeners. As I recalled in *Jazz Is*, "After a Cecil Taylor concert in California at which 3,000 people gave him standing ovations several times during the course of the performance, the distinguished [late] Los

Angeles critic Leonard Feather declared that 'anyone working with a jackhammer could have achieved the same results.' "

When I listen to Cecil, I do what one of his sidemen once advised: "You got to really open up to what Cecil's doing." I don't analyze. I get charged. One of his earlier sidemen, the remarkable bassist Buell Neidelinger, said to me recently: "After you've played with Cecil, how can you ever get that energy again?"

In the new, fifth edition, of the *Penguin Guide to Jazz*, Richard Cook and Brian Morton say of Cecil: "Throughout his career, both on and off the record, there has been no suspicion of any compromise at any point."

Long ago, Cecil said, "Part of what this music is about is not to be delineated exactly. It's about magic and capturing spirits."

He still gets, he tells me, his "most wonderful gigs" in Europe, and his best recordings, though he doesn't listen to what he's done, are on the German label FMP Records.

What keeps him going?

"I put my tragic energy into work."

Dizzy Gillespie:
Dizzy's Life Force Goes On

Years ago, a pianist recorded with Charlie Parker and Miles Davis. Now, at seventy-two, living alone, he was evicted from his apartment of nearly forty years. He couldn't pay the new rent. In shock, he collapsed and was hospitalized. Meanwhile, a city marshal put his instruments, belongings, sheet music, radio interviews, his life, in sixty garbage bags in the basement.

The Jazz Foundation of America's Emergency Fund workers went through all the bags and paid for a storage room to hold them. Wendy Oxenhorn, the Foundation's executive director, got him a keyboard so that, in the nursing home, he could be reunited with his music. He's now in a studio apartment, in an assisted-living building in Manhattan, with his piano, which he can play whenever he feels the spirit.

The Jazz Foundation has helped many more jazz musicians, some in urgent need, and it's now itself in need of more funds. This past June, 2001, the annual awards event of the jazz journalists Association was held at Birdland as a benefit for the Foundation.

Among others, I made a pitch for the Foundation, and during the exit music, several record company executives went over to Wendy Oxenhorn and pledged support. But more is needed, on a continuing basis, from others involved in jazz, including club owners—and listeners.

Present at the journalists' awards was Dr. Frank Forte, an internist, hematologist, and oncologist. He took care of Dizzy Gillespie when he was dying at Englewood Hospital in New Jersey.

"Dizzy had such a will to live," Forte told me, "all the way through. And it was not easy. He kept his wit, his humor. But he got very serious when he told me, 'I want you to take care of the musicians who haven't been as fortunate as I.'"

There is now a Dizzy Gillespie Institute at the hospital, where the Jazz Foundation—and its network of pro bono doctors—have, with donated funds, taken care of jazz musicians through heart surgery, cancer treatment, tests, and other medical care. Harlem Hospital is also involved.

Dizzy knew that most musicians don't get pensions or medical benefits, and they also need gigs when they're forgotten—not only for bread but for dignity. Wendy Oxenhorn reports: "Through a grant, we recently generated approximately $50,000 worth of gigs in the public schools in the month of April, employing many of our neediest musicians."

The Foundation often pays rents when needed, but this way, Oxenhorn continues, "they have a chance to pay their own rent and in the process, educate and introduce about 10,000 children to jazz."

Many of these older musicians are reluctant to ask for help, so a friend calls the Foundation. One musician, nearly eighty and disabled, had been subsisting on two cans of Slim Fast a day for a year and a half. Wendy told him that Meals on Wheels could bring him hot meals every day, but he said he didn't want anyone coming to his place. After four weeks of calls from Oxenhorn, he relented, and she soon got a message from him on her machine: "I feel like a new man, I got the life back in me again. Thank you for staying after me." (In a recent month, Oxenhorn says, "three musicians ended up at my place for dinner because they knew if they're hungry they can call and come on by.")

Forte has an idea to further Dizzy's desire to bring the life back to musicians trying to keep body and soul together. "In church," Forte told me, "there's a box, a collection box, for people in need. Why not have collection boxes for the Jazz Foundation in nightclubs where jazz is played?" Why not at record stores? And at concerts?

"What we do at, and through, the Foundation," Oxenhorn emphasizes, "is in no way a handout. It's a privilege to be of use to people who spent a lifetime giving us all they had. So many are now living alone without help, or with the constant threat of homelessness or untreated illnesses."

She tells of a drummer, a diabetic, who thought he had an infected toe; but a Foundation doctor took one look and had him instantly put in a hospital where he saved the drummer's leg from being amputated. "Without doctors," says Oxenhorn, "he probably would have died. Now all he lost was his toe. Sometimes we get lucky."

The Jazz Foundation of America is at 322 W. 48th Street, New York, NY 10036. Telephone: 212-245-3999. Toll free: 1-800-532-5267. All contributions are tax-deductible.

DICK WELLSTOOD:
SWINGING AT THE STICKET

Through the years, when Bill Buckley and I meet, we don't talk about politics. We talk about Dick Wellstood, a jazz pianist with resounding roots in stride piano who also played, in his unpredictable way, music by John Coltrane. Wellstood died ten years ago at the age of fifty-nine, but his most masterful solo piano recording, *Live at the Sticky Wicket*, is now available on Arbors Records (phone: 800-299-1930).

Bill Buckley, dba William F. Buckley Jr., founder of *National Review*, is a keyboardist (harpsichord division), and he is drawn to musicians who easily command all of the instrument but also bring grace and wit to the music. Dick Wellstood qualified on both counts, but he also brought an infectious joy to his improvising.

In conversation—when he wasn't engaged in fiercely competitive chess matches by mail—Wellstood was a wry, irreverent intellectual. In his music, he enjoyed continually surprising himself, while also surprising his listeners by suddenly changing the harmony, making the melody disappear and turning John Coltrane's "Giant

Steps" into a rag that Willie "The Lion" Smith might have played.

The Early Years

I first heard Wellstood some forty years ago in a band led by Bob Wilber, a pupil of Sidney Bechet. They had a long stay at the Savoy in Boston, a club in a black neighborhood with an unselfconsciously integrated clientele. The band itself had older black musicians and such young white players as the leader and Wellstood. The repertory was mostly jazz classics—Jelly Roll Morton's "The Pearls," for instance—from before the swing era.

The performances were rather archival, the musicians simulating rather than experiencing delight. Except for Wellstood, who made the Radcliffe girls and the listeners from the neighborhood applaud.

As the years went on, Wellstood became known for his mastery of stride piano, an exuberantly two-handed descendant of ragtime. But, as his longtime musical companion, Marty Grosz, points out, "Wellstood's restless imagination led him on beyond stride as well, into the precincts of blues, boogie-woogie, bebop, pop and rock."

As old-time jazz players used to say of musicians they admired, Wellstood had "big ears."

Wellstood's natural workplace was an informal club with informal customers who had no inhibitions about commenting out loud on the music as it was being played. He did not like to play in silence, respectful or otherwise.

It Happened One Night

A lively audience, eager for the pianist's daring improvisations, assembled on a November night in 1986 at the Sticky Wicket in Hopkinton, Massachusetts, not far from the traditional start of the Boston Marathon. The two-CD set from that night reminds me of a jazz truth I learned long ago. To carry an evening of solo piano requires not only exceptional musicianship but also a distinctive personality that infuses the music. Technical prowess by itself can be dull. Or, as Duke Ellington said one night to a young pianist, "My, you play so many notes."

"It took me six months," she told me later, "to realize what he meant: I wasn't saying anything."

Wellstood was one of the few solo pianists who could hold an audience for a whole evening. My own criterion for acute pleasure in any kind of music is when I suddenly shout aloud in delight. At some clubs, serious listeners are put off by such impertinence. But not, I sensed, at the Sticky Wicket. Anyway, I shouted often during this recital.

Wellstood being beyond categories, the repertory that night ranged from "Maple Leaf Rag" and "The Pearls" (he mentions memories of playing the tune in his youth at the Savoy) to songs by Fats Waller, Ellington, and Coltrane.

For much of the night, the rollicking mood conjured up memories of dances and rent-raising parties in Harlem long ago, but Wellstood was also—when he allowed himself to be—a romantic. So he played, with tender respect, such ballads as "How Long Has This Been Going On?"

Whatever the song, Wellstood's time, his beat, is unfailingly, viscerally compelling. He is one of those musicians who—if asked to demonstrate how not to swing—would find it difficult.

The clearest insight into the essence of Wellstood's approach to music is in a story by guitarist-singer Marty Grosz in the notes to *Live at the Sticky Wicket*:

"A trumpeter who was besotted with cornetist Bobby Hackett's exquisite melodic roulades once queried Dick, who had often accompanied Hackett, what it felt like to back the famous soloist.

"Dick thought for a moment and replied, 'Bobby is like a watchmaker who positions every screw, every ratchet, every jewel perfectly but to tell the truth, I'd rather play with Red Allen.'"

Henry "Red" Allen, originally from New Orleans, was a daring, unpredictable, showboating trumpet player who, although from another era, influenced Miles Davis. Although shy off the stand—as was Wellstood in a way—Red Allen specialized in boisterous interaction with his audiences and took great joy in the vocation that had chosen him.

Wellstood, who came out of Greenwich, Connecticut, not a notable source of hot jazzmen, was indeed at home when he played with the uninhibited trumpet player from New Orleans. But he was most free all by himself.

Jack Teagarden:
Teagarden Time

Recently, a reader called. He had come upon the deeply relaxing, blues-tinged trombone playing and singing of Jack Teagarden. The question was: "Is Teagarden black or white?"

I told him that in cultural historian Albert Murray's phrase, Teagarden could be called Omni-American. As Richard Sudhalter says in his exemplary notes for *The Complete Capitol Fifties Jack Teagarden Sessions* (Mosaic Records, telephone 203-327-7111), when the unassuming, young white Texan came to New York in 1927, "black musicians, chronically skeptical of white jazzmen in those musically segregated times, welcomed him in their midst—a few even hinting that no one who wasn't really black could play the blues that well."

Like Louis Armstrong, with whom he recorded some of the most mutually rejoicing affirmations of the life force of jazz, Teagarden radiated a natural, infectious warmth even before he picked up his horn. Off the stand, bassist Jack Lesberg recalled, Teagarden was "gentle, good-natured, never craved attention, just wanted to play and sing, and let life take care of the rest in whatever way it was going to."

Heaven With Armstrong

As a musician, he had so mastered his instrument that, according to trumpet player Don Goldie, "everything he played sounded inevitable. You couldn't imagine it ever being done any other way." And also like Armstrong, his singing and playing were seamless. He vocalized on trombone, and he sang with the same natural, flowing jazz time and melodic suppleness as on his horn.

He made every musical move sound easy; but trombonist-composer Bill Russo pointed out that Teagarden was so influential, because of his "range and flexibility," that he was "essentially responsible for a mature approach to trombone jazz."

His discography ranges from his four years with Paul Whiteman in the 1930s to sessions with Eddie Condon and recordings with his own small combos and big bands. Temperamentally unsuited to be in charge of a large enterprise and inept at financial details, Teagarden finally abandoned his attempts to direct an orchestra.

For the rest of his career he toured with a manageable number of musicians and became best known for his years as the primary sideman with Louis Armstrong from 1947 to 1951. "I'm really in heaven tonight," he said when he joined Armstrong.

I saw him often with Louis Armstrong, and so long as he was in musical conversations with his peers, Teagarden was content with who he was. At other times, however, life seemed less lofty. Mr. Sudhalter speaks of Teagarden's life-long "inner solitariness that never left him." And Mr. Goldie remembers a "feeling of sadness, that was always there."

Live at Monterey

The Mosaic box set consists of four CDs (76 tracks) he made for Capitol Records from 1955 to 1958 with various small combos and big bands. From the robust New Orleans classic "Muskrat Ramble" to the sensuously reflective ballad "Diane," a Teagarden signature for many years, his compelling personal way of telling a story confirms what his friend and frequent colleague cornetist Bobby Hackett said: "He was something that just happens once. It won't happen again. Not that way."

Teagarden's last recording—an indispensable part of his canon—was *A Hundred Years From Today: Jack Teagarden Family & Friends Live at the Monterey Jazz Festival, 1963.* It is available from the remarkably wide-ranging Memphis Archives (telephone 800-713-2150), whose catalog encompasses everything from songs played on board the Titanic to the music of imperial China to previously unreleased radio transcriptions by Art Tatum.

At Monterey, Jack Teagarden, who contributes a spoken introduction to each track, was reunited with his seventy-three-year-old pianist mother Helen, who encouraged him from the beginning and with whom he used to play in theaters for silent movies. Also present was his brother Charlie, a vigorous, incisive trumpet player, and his sister Norma, a pianist who, with Charlie, had often played in Jack's outfits.

Another long-time colleague on the stage at Monterey was the utterly singular clarinetist Pee Wee Russell, who first worked with Teagarden in the 1920s in a band led by the legendary Texas pianist Peck Kelley. From a younger generation was baritone saxophonist Gerry Mulligan, who greatly enjoyed jamming with his elders.

With aplomb, Mother Teagarden brings back to vigorous life two ragtime challenges for a two-handed virtuoso: "Tickled to Death" and "Possum & Taters." "That dear girl," says Jack, "you don't have to ask her twice."

Jack Teagarden is clearly delighted with this chance to play with both his family and old and new friends. Speaking of the family, he says, "It's the first time the four of us have been together for many years. I hope it won't be the last time."

Three and a half months later, Teagarden, alone in a New Orleans hotel room, died at age 59.

CARLA BLEY:
CARLA GOES HER OWN WAY

The music of some jazz players—John Coltrane, for example—is as serious as their lives. Others have been noted for their wit. Dizzy Gillespie, of course; Thelonious Monk; trombonist Vic Dickenson; pianist Jimmy Rowles; and Paul Desmond, the alto saxophonist who floated over Dave Brubeck's thunderous piano.

Carla Bley, an incorrigibly unpredictable composer, pianist and organist, has long been admired by many jazz musicians for her blithely satiric turns in such recordings as *Social Studies, Fancy Chamber Music* and *4X4* (all on her Watt label, now available on ECM Records.)

Merriment and parody, however, are not the only characteristics of her music. She works in many forms, small and large, and her scores for big jazz bands are matched only by those of Duke Ellington and the late Charles Mingus for yearning lyricism, explosive exultation, and other expressions of the human condition in between. Her free spirit encourages her soloists to expand their own voices and join her in surprising themselves. "I never give them any directions," she says. "I just give them the chord changes."

On *The Carla Bley Big Band Goes to Church*, recorded live in Italy, the writing ranges from meditation to jubilation. The impassioned soloists, such as trombonist Gary Valente, reminded me of the intense dialogues with God by the Jewish cantorial singers in my youthful attendance at Orthodox synagogues.

Another set I turn to when my spirits need raising is *The Carla Bley Big Band/European Tour 1997* (Watt). Her "Star-Spangled Banner Minor and Other Patriotic Songs" will, I expect, be an exuberantly irreverent obbligato when I next hear these anthems played straight, particularly with regard to her antic tribute to "La Marseillaise."

In *4X4* (Watt), recorded in 1999 in Oslo, an octet, playing her multicolored "Les Trois Lagons," recalled postmodernist jazzman Eric Dolphy telling me how, hearing birds outside his window, he brought them into his music. Ms. Bley composed this piece while living on an island in the Caribbean. As she and her longtime companion, bassist Steve Swallow, were playing duets in the evenings, "the birds and frogs seemed to sing along with us," and they too became part of the background to this composition, including "the two-note frog call."

Ms. Bley reminded me that I first knew her when she was the cigarette girl at the original Birdland in New York, standing as close to the bandstand as she could. She was nineteen. The music stayed with her, but she had to turn in the tips.

Born Carla Borg in Oakland, California, her own performances began when she was four, in church. She sang in the choir and played organ at weddings and funerals when she was able to reach the instrument. She tells me she was never able to fit in at school and dropped out in the tenth grade. As an instrumentalist and composer, she is—as she is pleased to acknowledge—self-taught.

In New York, in addition to her Birdland exposure to jazz luminaries, she worked as a coat-check girl at the Jazz Gallery, became part of the jazz scene as a composer and pianist, and married Paul Bley, an equally singular pianist and composer.

She later divorced Bley, and with trumpet player Michael Mantler formed the Jazz Composers Orchestra in 1964. Since then, she has appeared more often in Europe with her varied groups than in the United States. She also has a considerable following in Japan. Although she has received a Guggenheim Fellowship and a grant from the National Endowment for the Arts, most of her commissions have come from such European sources as the Berlin Contemporary Jazz Orchestra and the Grenoble Jazz Festival.

Her opera-oratorio, "Escalator Over the Hill"—a huge, two-hour sprawling fusion of jazz, rock and diverse ethnic echoes—has been staged in Cologne and in festivals in France, Austria, and Italy. Videotaped for French television, it was shown this February in Colorado during the annual Denver Jazz on Film Festival. The work, which requires immersion, is on ECM records. (Her recordings—there are twenty-three by now—are in many stores, or can be ordered from J&R Music, 1-800-221-8180, CD division.)

More accessible, along with the other CDs I've cited, is *Dinner Music*, recorded in Germany, and including "Sing

Me Softly of The Blues," which turns into an unexpected, rollicking celebration with trombonist Roswell Rudd, Carlos Ward on alto and tenor saxophone, and Bob Stewart on tuba.

Her "Dreams So Real" and "Dining Alone" in *Dinner Music* are tenderly introspective, with a characteristic sense of wonder. In "Dining Alone," she speaks as well as sings the lyrics, evoking a loneliness that is unaccountably hopeful. As in all her music, she is unfazed by seeming contradictions. She is also her own record producer, having formed her Watt label when no one else would record her, and she still is wholly in control. But her sense of fun is intact.

She found school boring because there was no fun in it, and her intent in life has been to find new sources of enjoyment in music—as when she added six classical musicians, members of the English Chamber Orchestra Opus 20, to her big band for a tour of Britain. The audiences, she reports, also had fun in the combination and "tried hard not to applaud in the wrong places."

Carla Bley did not appear in Ken Burns' "Jazz" on television, but a producer might enjoy presenting this tall, striking woman, with her mane of blonde hair and her carousel of surprises. Asked to name her best work, she gives the same answer Duke Ellington did: "It isn't happening yet."

WYCLIFFE GORDON:
THE TALKING TROMBONE

At thirty-six, Wycliffe Gordon, who became internationally known as a member of Wynton Marsalis's Lincoln Center Jazz Orchestra, has entered the pantheon of jazz trombonists—nearly all of whom he has studied from the time a great aunt bequeathed the twelve-year-old in Waynesboro, Georgia, a five-record anthology of jazz.

"I heard slave chants, ragtime, Jelly Roll Morton, all the way up to Duke Ellington," Mr. Gordon told me. But what most strongly attracted him was Louis Armstrong's Hot Seven recording of "Keyhole Blues." It was "Pops's silvery, singing sound, and so much feeling he put into his music."

Mr. Gordon's was a musical home. His father was a classical pianist and teacher, and both parents spent a lot of time in church. But unlike Mahalia Jackson, for instance—another influence on Gordon—they also enjoyed secular music, particularly the blues.

Of all the trombonists of his generation, Mr. Gordon is abidingly immersed in the entire jazz tradition. His own playing is immediately—often exuberantly—identifiable, but on trombone, he is an authority on the styles of Jack Teagarden, Trummy Young, Al Grey, Vic Dickenson, Dicky Wells, and Lawrence Brown, a longtime soloist with Duke Ellington's orchestra.

"Many trombonists," Mr. Gordon says, "play like a trumpet or a saxophone, but Brown understood the true character of his instrument. When he played, it was as if he was singing." Mr. Gordon, through his mastery of various mutes and plungers, also talks through his horn—a skill he began to learn from the growls of Ellington's trumpet player, Bubber Miley, and Duke's sly, witty trombonist, "Tricky Sam" Nanton.

Mr. Gordon started on trombone when he was twelve, and while in high school in Augusta, Georgia—as he told jazz critic Ted Panke—"I connected with the idea that you can try to sing through the instrument," as Lawrence Brown did. And with the feeling in the voices he heard in church.

A proud member of McDonald's All-American High School Marching Band, Mr. Gordon went on to Florida A & M University in Tallahassee, a school known for its marching band. There, Wynton Marsalis, teaching at a clinic in 1987, heard him. In 1989, Gordon joined Marsalis's Septet, and early in their association, the leader-educator gave the fledgling jazzman a list of recordings to buy.

Thereupon, Mr. Gordon's influences came to include Thelonious Monk, John Coltrane, guitarist Charlie Christian, and trombonists J.J. Johnson and Curtis Fuller. But he never lost the joyous spirit he first experienced in Louis Armstrong—as can be heard in all of Gordon's CDs, and particularly in the song "New Awlins" (on *Slidin' Home*, Nagel Heyer Records, www.nagelheyer.com; also available in many record stores).

Gordon plays with the contagious jubilation I heard long ago in the music of New Orleans trombonist Jim Robinson at Preservation Hall. "I like to see people happy," Robinson used to say, "and then the spirit gets to me and I can make my trombone sing. When I play sweet music, I try to give my feelings to the other fellow too." Mr. Gordon could have naturally joined a session in Preservation Hall.

The range of Mr. Gordon's feelings—not only in his playing but also in his equally distinctive compositions and arrangements—can be heard in *The Search* (Nagel Heyer) and the often rapturous Criss Cross CD, *The Gospel Truth*, (www.crisscrossjazz.com), with singer Carrie Smith and Mr. Gordon's customary associates, mostly from the Lincoln Center Jazz Orchestra. Continually personal and passionate are trumpet player Marcus Printup, pianist Eric Reed, and Victor Goines on tenor, clarinet, and baritone saxophone.

Mr. Gordon no longer tours with the Lincoln Center Jazz Orchestra, though he still appears with it in concerts. He heads his own group in engagements here and abroad, as well as teaching in clinics. He is now also an associate professor at Michigan State University in East Lansing, where he teaches jazz studies, is in charge of the jazz band, and is involved in shaping the curriculum.

"When we were on the road years ago," Mr. Gordon told me recently, "we'd talk about whether jazz would ever become part of any curriculum, even at the college level."

While his position at Michigan State is fulltime, Mr. Gordon says that he will continue to travel and perform because "at this school, they want you to teach what you *do*."

When I first got to know jazz musicians—Duke Ellington, Rex Stewart and, later, Dizzy Gillespie and John Coltrane—I was struck by how much many of them knew beyond music as a result of their travels. "I read the columnists on foreign affairs," Ellington once told me, "but I already know a lot of what they're saying because I've already been there."

And Mr. Gordon, during an interview in the notes for *The Gospel Truth*, says: "I was brought up in the Southern Black Baptist church, and being able to travel and see places and meet people I read about in college history or humanities classes opened my mind to the way things actually are in the world. I learned to deal with different religious and spiritual beliefs, to accept different musical forms and sounds, and utilize them to develop my own way of playing. When you travel, you discover something Louis Armstrong knew about everyone in the world—we all have the same needs."

In his notes to Wycliffe Gordon's *Slidin' Home*, Wynton Marsalis says: "Jazz music set musicians and listeners around the world free to be themselves in public"—as their knowledge of themselves kept growing. And Mr. Marsalis writes of Mr. Gordon: "He makes the trombone talk, growl, mutter, moan, cry, sigh, squeal, exclaim, proclaim, and defame." And he can make even "Danny Boy" sound freshly poignant.

Louis Armstrong:
They Would Beat Jesus
if He Was Black and Marched

To the young jazz musicians in the blazing orbit of Charlie Parker and Dizzy Gillespie in the 1950s and 1960s, Louis Armstrong was of another time. Oh, he sure could swing, but you could always tell what the melody was. The harmonies were hardly challenging, and as for his swinging, well, those modernists would say, there's more to jazz than being able to pat your foot to the music.

Worst of all, many of them charged, Armstrong as a performer was pretty close to an Uncle Tom—always grinning, with that big white handkerchief.

Back then, Dizzy Gillespie, already a bebopper of renown, spoke of Armstrong's "plantation image." But by 1970, Gillespie, at the Newport Festival, changed his tune: "If it hadn't been for him, there wouldn't have been none of us. I want to thank Louis Armstrong for my livelihood."

Miles Davis, never one to salute an Uncle Tom, concurred: "Louis has been through all kinds of styles.

You know you can't play anything on a horn Louis hasn't played."

By that time, much of the jazz world was aware of what this "handkerchief-head"—as some young blacks used to call him—had said very publicly in 1957 about how Arkansas governor Orville Faubus had defied the Supreme Court and was preventing black students from enrolling in the Little Rock public schools.

"The way they are treating people in the South," Louis told the press, "the government can go to hell!" As for the popular president, Dwight Eisenhower, who said he had no brief for "the extremists on either side" of that conflict, Armstrong said: "The President has no guts!"

As soon as that story broke, Armstrong's manager, the volcanic Joe Glaser, sent an emissary to Louis on the road to order him to shut up because that kind of talk was bad for business. Louis threw the emissary out of his dressing room.

In 1965, when television stations around the world were showing the brutal beatings by local and state police on ecumenical members of Martin Luther Kings' march on Selma, Alabama, Louis—playing in Copenhagan—said, after watching the blood of marching blacks and whites flow on television: "They would beat Jesus if he was black and marched."

When they were stereotyping Louis Armstrong as a kind of Mantan Moreland years before, some young black musicians were unaware of Armstrong's intimacy with Jim Crow. As bassist George "Pop" Foster, who was on the road with Armstrong in the South during the 1930's, recalled:

"If you had a colored bus driver back then, they'd lock you up in every little country town for 'speeding.' It was very rough trying to find a place to sleep in the South. You couldn't get into the hotel for whites, and the colored didn't have any hotels. You rented places in private homes, boardinghouses, and whorehouses. The food was awful and we tried to find places where we could cook. We carried a bunch of pots and pans with us."

By 1960, after Armstrong had triumphantly toured several continents, he was on the road again in his native land. Also on the bus was the already renowned photographer, Herb Snitzer. He recalls:

"We set out on a bright, warm Saturday afternoon, headed north, with everybody in a good mood. The bus did not have a toilet. So somewhere in Connecticut, we stopped in order for Louis to go to the bathroom. I was stunned when the owner of the restaurant, clearly on the basis of race, refused him use of otherwise available facilities. I will never forget the look on Louis's face. Here he was, a favorite to millions of people, American's single most identifiable entertainer, and yet excluded in the most humiliating fashion from a common convenience."

Some ten years before, I interviewed Armstrong backstage at Symphony Hall in Boston. He was bone-tired, having finished a characteristically long concert, never coasting because he enjoyed satisfying his audiences. But he was free with his midnight time, and he talked mostly of race. He was not grinning, but he was not bitter. Sad and hurt. But he knew he had triumphed over all that bigotry. As Dizzy Gillespie said around that time, the

Armstrong grin represented Louis's "absolute refusal to let anything, even anger about racism, steal the joy from his life."

"When I pick up that horn," Louis once told Gilbert Millstein of the *New York Times*, "that's all. The world's behind me, and I don't concentrate on nothing but that horn. I mean, I don't feel no different about that horn now than I did when I was playing in New Orleans. That's my living and my life. I love them notes. That's why I try to make them right."

Also, he often spoke about musicians, and other friends, who had taught him throughout his life that he couldn't stereotype whites as many of them had stereotyped him.

When he was very young, Louis worked for a Jewish family in New Orleans, the Karmofskys. He had been blowing a tin horn and saw in a pawn shop window, a cornet for five dollars. The Karmofskys lent him the money to buy the horn, his first real instrument.

Mrs. Karmofsky insisted that Louis eat dinner with the family, and—as Gary Giddins writes in *Satchmo* (Da Capo Press)—"Mrs. Karmofsky taught him to sing 'Russian Lullaby.'" It was, Louis remembered, "so soft and sweet. Then [they] bid each other good night. They were always warm and kind to me. . . . When I reached the age of eleven," as Giddins quotes Louis, "I began to realize it was the Jewish family who instilled in me singing from the heart."

And Louis knew—despite that restaurant owner in Connecticut—changes were taking place. In a letter to jazz critic Leonard Feather (in *Louis Armstrong in His Own Words: Selected Writings*, edited by Thomas Brother (Oxford University Press), Louis said:

"I'd like to recall one of my most inspiring moments. I was playing a concert date in a Miami auditorium. I walked on stage and there I saw something I'd never seen. I saw thousands of people, colored and white, on the main floor. Not segregated in one row of whites and another row of Negroes. Just all together—naturally. I thought I was in the wrong state. When you see things like that, you know you're going forward."

Louis provided considerable momentum to that forward motion. The late Charles Black, a longtime professor of law at Yale University and later Columbia University, was a key member of Thurgood Marshall's legal team which won a series of victories against segregated schools that climaxed in *Brown v. Board of Education* (1954), in which the Supreme Court ruled unanimously that segregated public schools are inherently unconstitutional.

Black used to tell of how, as a youngster in Texas, growing up racist, like his friends, he went to hear a trumpet player named Louis Armstrong at a dance in Texas. Armstrong stunned him with the fire, lyricism, and grandeur of his playing. The stereotypes of blacks cracked, and Charles Black said later that hearing Armstrong put him on the path to his subsequent work with Thurgood Marshall.

Louis Armstrong knew the power and depth of his music. He liked to tell this story:

"I'm playin' a date in Florida, livin' in the colored section and I'm playin' my horn for *myself* one afternoon. A knock come on the door and there's an old, gray-haired flute player from the Philadelphia Orchestra down there for his health. Walking through that neighborhood, he heard this horn, playing *Cavalleria Rusticana*, which he said he had never heard phrased like that before. To him it was as if an orchestra was behind it."

Armstrong was once asked by Ruby Braff—a cornet player much influenced by Armstrong and now arguably the most melodically imaginative improviser on his horn—how he was able to sound so compelling, even when his backing was not at all up to his musicianship.

"When that happens," Armstrong told his disciple, "I put what's going on behind me out of my mind, and I have in my head a wonderful orchestra accompanying me."

The music that Charles Black heard and that ignited audiences in Europe, Africa, and across this land had the same impact that cornetist Rex Stewart—who became a singular soloist with Duke Ellington's orchestra—described when Louis first came to New York from Chicago in 1924 to join the mighty band of Fletcher Henderson:

"We had never heard anybody improvise that way before—the brilliance and boldness of his ideas, the fantastic way he developed them, the deepness of his swing, and that gloriously full, clear sound. It was stunning! I went mad with the rest of the musicians. I tried to walk like him, talk like him, eat like him, sleep like him."

And Roy Eldridge ("Little Jazz") who always played with such intensity that it was as if he felt it was the last solo he would ever create, said of first hearing Armstrong:

"He started out like a new book, building and building, chorus after chorus, and finally reaching a full climax— right, clean, and clear. The rhythm was rocking, and he had that sound going along with it. Everybody was standing up, including me."

Clarinetist Edmond Hall, also from New Orleans, was on the road with Louis for a long time during the years when some of the "modern" jazz musicians were putting Louis down as just an entertainer.

"There'd be times," Edmond told me one night after a gig, "when, even on a number I'd heard so often, Louis's sound would just get *cracking* and I'd get goose pimples."

In 1931, after Louis had startled not only musicians but listeners and dancers in New York and Chicago, he came home to New Orleans where he was booked into a club where no black band had performed before.

On opening night, Louis picked up his horn and waited for the station's staff announcer to introduce him. But that Southerner couldn't do it. Within Louis's hearing, he said that he would not "announce that nigger man."

Armstrong turned to the band, signaled for an emphatic chord, and announced the show himself. Louis later told his first biographer—the Belgian critic and enthusiast, Robert Goffin—"It was the first time that a Negro *spoke* on the radio down there."

Now, the city of New Orleans, a hundred years—or a hundred and one, depending on which biographer you read—after Louis's death, has moved to name the city's airport after Louis Armstrong.

As I've written in *Jazz Is* (Random House/Limelight Edition): "Not long before Louis died, a young trumpeter and I were in a huge hotel room where Louis was playing. After jiving and scat singing through 'Mack The Knife,' Louis moved into his theme song, 'When It's Sleepy Time Down South.'

"Staying close to the melody, Louis was subtly adding a new dimension to the song, a chilling and yet exhilarating fusion of poignancy and strength.

"There were tears in the eyes of the musician standing next to me. 'Man,' he said, 'Pops makes you feel so *good*.'"

As you can hear in the Columbia/Legacy *Louis Armstrong: The Complete Hot Five* and *Hot Seven Recordings*, and *Louis Armstrong Plays W.C. Handy*. Also, *Louis Armstrong/Satchmo: A Musical Autobiography*, with narration by Louis (Verve).

LOUIS ARMSTRONG:
DON'T LET ANYBODY TELL
YOU LOUIS IS DEAD!

On the bright, crisp morning of October 15, Jon Faddis stood on the balcony of the Louis Armstrong House in Corona, Queens—outside Louis' den. With customary clarity and aplomb he played Louis' a cappella chorus on "West End Blues" to officially open this National Historic Landmark and New York City Landmark. The block, now named Louis Armstrong Place, was jammed with Louis' longtime neighbors and their schoolkids, musicians and people of all colors, ages, and classes from this country, Germany, Poland, and other lands reached by Louis' horn, voice, and spirit.

Further animating the celebration was eighty-five-year-old Phoebe Jacobs, vice president of the Louis Armstrong Educational Foundation, and a vital figure on the New York jazz scene for the fifty years I've been part of it, and before. Phoebe, a close friend of Louis and Lucille Armstrong, commanded the crowd: "Don't let anybody tell you Louis is dead. He's not!"

Jon Faddis, speaking of the depth of Louis' impact, told of when Armstrong, in 1953, came to play in the Belgian Congo where, as is not unusual there, a fierce civil war was underway. "The factions," said Jon, "stopped the war to listen to Louis' music. We could definitely use Louis Armstrong now." As Stanley Crouch of the Louis Armstrong Educational Foundation added, "He was a man who represented America as well as it has ever been represented."

The redbrick house, which Lucille Armstrong bought in 1943, was seen for the first, utterly surprising time by Louis when he came off one of his long road trips. He lived there until he died on July 6, 1971, in the master bedroom's wall-to-wall bed. He never wanted to leave the neighborhood, where his home was of the same modest scale as the other houses in that section of Corona.

Selma Heraldo, who lived in the house next door for eighty years, told *Newsday*: "I didn't regard him as a celebrity, just a plain human being. He told me he came from poor and didn't believe in putting on airs." Louis often sat on the front steps, playing his horn for the neighborhood kids, and when the ice-cream man came by, Louis did the right thing by the boys and girls. In Queens, named after Armstrong are P.S. 143 and middle school I.S. 227. Every morning in the latter school, the kids begin the day serenaded by Louis' recording of "What a Wonderful World."

Inside the Louis Armstrong House, visitors can hear, in three of the rooms, excerpts from Louis' expansive collection of recorded tapes, with their personally decorated boxes. (They can also be heard at satchmo.net). At the Louis Armstrong Archives at Queens College (718-997-3670, www.satchmo.net), six rooms contain Louis' lovingly assembled collection of 1,600 recordings; 650 reel-to-reel tapes with his collages on the boxes; eighty-six scrapbooks; thousands of photographs, along with correspondence, manuscripts, scores of awards, and five trumpets.

Louis funded and founded the Louis Armstrong Educational Foundation in 1969. ("I wanted to give back to the world some of the goodness the world gave to me.") It has provided financial support for a wide-ranging variety of educational projects in schools, including scholarships. There is also the Louis Armstrong Music Therapy Program, at the pediatric center of Beth Israel Hospital in New York.

Louis believed in the healing powers of music. "He once told me," Jacobs recalls, "to send some recordings to an insane asylum in New Orleans. Not just *his* recordings, but a variety of recordings, including classical music. And he also had recordings sent to a labor room in a hospital." He wanted to nurture women's spirits as they were giving birth.

The Louis Armstrong House is at 34-56 107th Street, Corona Queens, New York, NY 11368 (718-478-8274 and satchmo.net for information on guided tours, hours, and the gift shop). An invaluable guide to the house and to Louis, in and out of the house, is *Louis Armstrong: The Offstage Story of Satchmo* (Collectors Press Inc., P.O. Box 230986, Portland, OR 97281. 800-423-1848, collectors-press.com). The author is Michael Cogswell, director of the Louis Armstrong House & Archives, Queens College. Future generations will owe a large debt to Cogswell for the dedication he has given to preserving these dimensions of Louis' legacy.

Among the stories, correspondence, and photos from Louis' private collection in the book, there is this Armstrong quote from 1957 when Arkansas Governor Orville Faubus was preventing black children from entering Little Rock public schools in defiance of the Supreme Court while President Dwight Eisenhower hesitated to intervene. Louis publicly called Faubus "an uneducated plowboy," and said of Eisenhower that he was "two-faced" and "had no guts." Later, Louis canceled an official U.S. tour of the Soviet Union: "The way they're treating my people in the South, the government can go to hell."

As Crouch said as the ribbon was cut on the entrance to the Louis Armstrong House: "Louis had that pure human feeling." All of it.

WOODY HERMAN:
WOODY HERMAN'S DOWN-HOME,
PERSONAL BLUES

Woody Herman is best known as the leader of the various blazing Herman Herds that starred such legends of modern jazz as tenor saxophonists Stan Getz and Zoot Sims, trombonist Bill Harris, and drummer Don Lamond. But their predecessors in Herman's first jazz venture, The Band That Plays the Blues, are barely mentioned by present-day jazz chroniclers, and the band itself has been largely forgotten.

I was fourteen when I heard "Woodchopper's Ball" (1939), and two years later, the haunting "Blue Flame," along with a singular "Blues in the Night," with its composer, Harold Arlen, singing counterpoint to Woody Herman's vocal.

At long last, Naxos, a classical label with a new Naxos Jazz Legends line of astutely selected reissues (Coleman Hawkins, Sidney Bechet, Teddy Wilson), has restored that sound I heard so long ago on *Woody Herman: The Band That Plays the Blues (1937–1941)*. With all respect to the boisterous later Herds, these jazzmen created, for nine years, the most abidingly satisfying Woody Herman recordings.

Bebopper Dizzy Gillespie wrote a score for the band in 1942. Woody always had what musicians called "big ears," and Dizzy later said of Woody: "Here's a guy that went through all the eras of jazz almost from the beginning and stayed fresh. He stuck with it."

It was in 1936 that Herman started a co-operative blues band with—for a while—every decision made in committee. For its first gig in Brooklyn, the sidemen got $50 a week and the leader $75. At first, the band had a rocky time on the road. Woody told Gene Lees in the definitive biography, "Leader of the Band: Woody Herman" (Oxford University Press):

"The blues were the best things we knew how to play, but we had to do a lot of fighting to play them. The managements preferred . . . fox trots, rumbas and waltzes . . . to satisfy the dancers."

During an engagement in a Texas hotel, the boss sent the white leader a note: "Would you please stop playing this nigger music."

But Woody stuck with it, regenerated by the large, continuous record sales of his theme, "Woodchopper's Ball." The band didn't play only blues, but those of his original Decca recordings represented on this Naxos set gave the band its identity.

Woody, a clarinetist, alto saxophonist and singer, had come out of the popular Isham Jones orchestra, a band that definitely did not play the blues. On his own, Woody assembled players who—like the Count Basie sidemen—

were not profligate with notes and daring harmonies. Among those letting the music breathe were Joe Bishop on flugelhorn, trumpet player Cappy Lewis, guitarist Hy White, trombonist Neil Reid, and drummer Frankie Carlson. It was an ensemble band, with soloists seamlessly emerging over a beat that flowed as naturally as the blues.

As a clarinetist, Woody Herman never provided competition to Benny Goodman, Artie Shaw or the literally inimitable Pee Wee Russell. But his sound was warm and evocatively yearning. When his later bands were composed of daredevils shaped by the boldly new language of Charlie Parker and Gillespie, the leader's clarinet playing was not only dwarfed but often sounded miscast as the fleeter, proudly hip improvisers roared past him.

Though seldom emphasized any longer in treatises on jazz singers, Woody—even with his later postswing-era Herdsmen—was a compelling storyteller. On this reissue set, he creates penetrating, sometimes eerie moods on "Calliope Blues" and "Riverbed Blues." But always, the feeling—clearly indebted to black blues bards but very personal—is down home, as blues men used to say.

The Band That Plays the Blues startled many of its admirers, including me, by hiring a woman trumpet player. There were swinging female horn players in the International Sweethearts of Rhythm and other all-women bands, and though the more renowned mainstream leaders had girl singers out front, no women played in the brass and reed sections.

Hearing of trumpeter Billie Rogers's arrival in 1941, after these recordings were made, I went to a Woody Herman engagement at a Boston theater—the band performed before the feature film—wondering if this chick, the term of the time, could hold her own with these deep swingers. The twenty-two-year-old from Montana, of all places, didn't miss a cue or a beat.

One of the sidemen, embarrassed to be on the same stand with a woman, resigned. This did not seem to faze Rogers. Woody recalled that when the band played five or six theater shows a day, she had more stamina than the rest of the section. Mr. Lees writes that she "always gave Woody credit for courage in opening the way for other women to follow." Yet to this day the world-traveling Lincoln Center Jazz Orchestra does not have a permanent woman member—unlike the Smithsonian Jazz Masterworks Orchestra in Washington. Jazzwomen demonstrating recently outside Lincoln Center held aloft a sign addressed to women-free ensembles: "Testosterone is not a musical instrument." Woody wasn't mentioned.

In his fifties, he was still on the road for fifty weeks a year. But the hard rains of the blues changed the rest of his life when it was discovered by the Internal Revenue Service that his manager, Abe Turchen, a compulsive gambler, had not paid Herman's income and withholding taxes on the musicians' salaries for three years. Woody was presented with a bill for $1.6 million.

Woody was stunned, and it only grew worse as many other creditors not paid by Turchen emerged. When

Woody became ill and there were no more of his earnings for the IRS to continually confiscate, the government seized his home in October, 1987. He left in an ambulance and died, at seventy-four, later that month.

His death occurred almost exactly fifty years after he had hit his peak. In 1937, the year-old Band That Plays the Blues was challenged by Count Basie's band at the Roseland Ballroom in New York. Basie and his men were new to the city, but Basie later said, without excuses, "The only band that ever cut my band was the Woody Herman band" swinging the blues.

NORMAN GRANZ:
GOODBYE MY FRIEND

There is no one in the history of jazz," Clark Terry told me, "who has had more respect for the musicians than Norman [Granz]. Once, a lot of his regular troops—Ella Fitzgerald, Dizzy Gillespie, Benny Carter and me, among them—were booked into a place in Italy where they didn't have a dressing room. We had to dress out in the cold. The producer couldn't understand why we looked so upset. Norman simply said, 'Okay, let's split.' As we left, the promoter was screaming about suing Granz, and Norman said in that deadly way of his, 'Go ahead. I don't expose my people to this kind of treatment.'"

Norman also respected listeners. "When I gave a concert," he told me, "I had an obligation to the man who bought a ticket. As a result, the first thing I did was ban all photographers who would rush up during the show to get what they called 'good shots.' The second thing is—and this happened every time I knew there was an auxiliary use, television or recording—I never let that thing be primary. The best concert was an uninterrupted concert that built as the musicians could make it build."

And he had respect for future listeners. "At Verve," Norman recalled, "my bookkeeper would invariably say, 'Well, why do you want to put out Roy Eldridge?' Or, 'Why do you want to put out Ben Webster? They don't sell.' And I'd say, 'Well, whether they sell or not, they're important, they should be recorded and they're what Verve stands for, so we don't have to discuss that any further.' "

Norman died November 22, 2001, at age eighty-three in Geneva of complications from cancer, but his legacy to jazz will survive forever. Imagine what the living history of jazz would be like without all the recordings Norman made. In 1954 I wrote in *Down Beat*: "Granz, more than any other single force in jazz . . . has consistently supported those artists that form the mainstream of the jazz tradition—artists whose roots are life-deep in jazz and without whom there would have been no modern jazz, cool or turbulent."

Much as been written about the arrest by Houston detectives of Norman and Jazz at the Philharmonic musicians backstage on October 7, 1955. As always, Norman had insisted that there would be no audience segregation at the concert. He himself removed the "white" and "Negro" signs in the auditorium.

There were to be two shows that night, and after the first, the musicians were playing cards in the dressing room. Three detectives, claiming to be life-long jazz fans, burst in, took the money on the floor and arrested everybody. As the cops moved toward the bathroom, Norman blocked their way. "What are you doing here?" one of the detectives asked. "Watching you," Norman answered. "I want to make sure you're not going to plant something."

"I ought to kill you," said the detective, pressing his revolver into Granz's stomach.

"Well," Norman said, "if you're going to shoot me, I mean, shoot me."

The cop said they were all going to be taken down to the station house. Norman pointed out that 3,000 tickets had been sold for the second show. "You're going to have the biggest uprising you've ever had," he told the detectives, "because I'm going to go out on stage and tell them the concert is cancelled, and then I'm going to tell them why it's cancelled."

A compromise was reached. Norman, Ella, Dizzy, Illinois Jacquet, and Ella's assistant were arrested with the promise they'd be back for the second show. They were in the station house for half an hour. Besieged by the press, Dizzy was asked his name. He said, "Louis Armstrong," and that's how it appeared in the papers. Norman paid the $50 bail and they went back to the auditorium, but first a detective asked Ella for her autograph.

Norman paid for the best lawyer he could find; the charges were dismissed. And Norman got the bail money back.

As Jon Thurber wrote in his first-rate *Los Angeles Times* obituary of Granz, Norman's credo was: "If you don't get substantially what you want, be ready to walk. And don't look back."

I often interviewed Norman and the musicians who traveled with him. Parts of some of those articles are in

Let Freedom Swing: Norman Granz and Jazz at the Phil-harmonic, 1944–1957—a thesis for a master of arts degree at George Mason University by Tad Hershorn, who is now the archivist at the Institute of Jazz Studies. I'm grateful to Tad for preserving the stories.

John Coltrane:
The Spoken Essence

Having grown up on Lester Young, Coleman Hawkins, Buddy Tate, and Don Byas, it took me some time to be drawn into John Coltrane's universe. In *Down Beat*, at first, I wrote of his unappealing sound on records, and in clubs I tended to lose my way in his long dense solos. But Don Ayler, Albert's trumpet-playing brother, gave me some useful advice. He was talking about how to get inside what his brother was doing; but it also opened me up to other path breakers. "Don't always focus on the notes," Don Ayler said, "on what sequence they'd be in if you were to write them down. Instead try to move your imagination toward the sound. Follow the sound; the pitches, the colors. You have to almost watch them move. You have to try to listen to everything together."

It worked all the more so, as I came to listen to Coltrane talk about what he was endlessly searching for. At first, he resisted speaking about his music. I'd call and say that I'd been asked to write the liner notes for one of his new recordings. And Coltrane would say, "I wish you wouldn't. If the music can't stand on its own, what's the use?" As the next step in the ritual, I would say, "But John, it's a gig." And he, being a kind man, would sigh, "All right, what do you want to ask?"

About those long, dervishlike solos, I suggested one afternoon that maybe he was trying to so envelop the listener that all other distractions would disappear and, in the total immersion, the listener would no longer analyze but become the music. "That may be a secondary effect," John said, "but I'm not consciously trying to do that. I'm still primarily looking into certain sounds, certain scales. Not that I'm sure of what I'm looking for, except that it'll be something that hasn't been played before. I don't know what it is. I know I'll have that feeling when I get it. When things are constantly happening, the pieces just don't feel that long."

But what he was searching for, continually, was something more elusive, as mysterious as the meaning, the mission, of his later years. Back then, Dizzy Gillespie told me, "All music has been out there, from the beginning of time, and you're lucky if you can get a small piece of it." To Coltrane, however, music—his reason for being in music—was to become part of the source of consciousness from the beginning of time. This was hard for me—a facts-on-the-ground atheist—to follow at first. But as Coltrane and I had more conversations, I began to understand, within my limits.

He spoke of Om or Aum. In the Hindu and Buddhist systems of belief, it means (according to the unabridged *American Heritage Dictionary*), "the supreme and most sacred syllable, consisting in Sanskrit of the three sounds (a), (u), and (m), representing various fundamental triads and believed to be the spoken essence of the universe." To John, Om was "the first vibration—that sound, that spirit which set everything else into being," and he wanted to connect, to enter into, that universal, transcendent peace. To keep trying to get there, he, through his music, had to continue to search deeper and deeper into himself and exorcise his own dissonances, his own demons—as you can hear in "Ascension," among others of his later recordings. Marion Brown, who was on the "Ascension" date, said both takes "had that kind of thing in them that makes people scream. The people in the studio were screaming."

And so John, who studied yoga and read the Bhagavad-Gita, kept learning new instruments with their overtones of being; listened to recordings of South African pygmies and, of course, the multiple dimensions of time (including distinct times of the day and night) in Indian music. When I asked him why he wanted two drummers, and sometimes two bassists, with him, he said patiently, "Because I want more of the sense of the expansion of time. I want the time to be more plastic." Or, as T. S. Eliot wrote: "Time present and time past/Are both perhaps present in time future/And time future contained in time past."

I expect that by now, the millions of listeners to Coltrane around the world don't know, and don't have to know, the ultimate light he was pursuing. But since he did tell me, I thought I would pass it on for anyone who wants to know. At the end of one conversation, John—talking more to himself than to me—said: "I wish I could walk up to my music as if the first time, as if I had never heard it before. Being so inescapably a part of it, I'll never know what the listener gets, what the listener feels, and that's too bad."

That was knowledge he could never get; but he did know—from their total, shouting involvement in his music during live performances—that he was reaching deep into listeners, whether Om was present or not.

DAVE McKENNA:
KING OF THE TWO-HANDS

There have been few jazz pianists with the taste, exhilaration and two-handed technique to command attention on their own—with neither rhythm section nor horns. Among them have been Willie "The Lion" Smith, Fats Waller, Duke Ellington (while he was waiting for the band to assemble), Art Tatum (more a whirlwind than a storyteller) and Thelonious Monk.

Lesser known, except among musicians, is seventy-one-year-old Dave McKenna, whom the *New Yorker's* Whitney Balliett has called "the hardest-swinging pianist of all time." But Mr. McKenna can also tenderly illuminate a ballad.

In March of this year, thirty-six-year-old Bill Charlap, emerging as a candidate for the pantheon of jazz keyboardists, instantly recognized Mr. McKenna during a *Down Beat* Blindfold Test: "(He) sounds like two pianists; there's so much definition between his right hand and left hand. . . . He'll whip up something perfect right to the bottom of the keyboard. That's as great as solo piano ever was."

Mr. McKenna is heard in the recently released *An Intimate Evening With Dave McKenna*, on Arbors Records (www.arborsrecords.com), in a recording of a 1999 concert at the Opera House in Sarasota, Florida. As Gunnar Jacobsen writes in the notes: "The audience was filled with musicians, something which usually happened at his appearances."

From the opening Original Dixieland Jazz Band romp "Fidgety Feet" to the dreamlike "It's the Last Dance," Mr. McKenna's orchestral piano is so fulfilling and sometimes overwhelming that, after the concert, a woman told the soloist he had moved her to tears. "I played that bad," he said, smiling. Having listened to the recording often, I find that Mr. McKenna lifts me above the turmoil of global news to a touch of hope for the human condition.

Mr. McKenna, not given to self-aggrandizement, calls himself "a saloon pianist, a song player." Born in Woonsocket, Rhode Island, in 1930, he joined the musicians' union when he was fifteen, having already included in his repertory appropriate songs for bridal showers and weddings. Four years later, he went on the road with Charlie Ventura, moving on to play with Woody Herman, Bobby Hackett, Stan Getz, and other jazz groups.

By 1966, having moved to Cape Cod, Mr. McKenna increasingly worked as a soloist, and sometimes with small combos. For nine years, six nights a week, Mr. McKenna made the Plaza Bar at Boston's Copley Plaza Hotel a meeting place for visiting musicians. As Mr. Jacobsen notes, "Tony Bennett and many others would stop by and sit in for a song. Oscar Peterson, George Shearing, Bill Evans" and numerous other renowned pianists came to hear Mr. McKenna continually regenerate his vast repertory.

Learning From the Horn

Mr. McKenna's favorite pianist was Nat Cole. "He could come closer," Mr. McKenna told me, "than any other piano player to bending notes like a horn player. And his swing was unstoppable." But Mr. McKenna's main influences were horn players, among them Louis Armstrong, Benny Goodman, Artie Shaw, Johnny Hodges, Bobby Hackett, Dizzy Gillespie, Charlie Parker, and Miles Davis.

"Whatever Louis played," Mr. McKenna says, "it could be tomorrow. His music is timeless, always relevant." In addition to the Arbors set of the Florida concert, McKenna has recorded a series of equally timeless solo performances for Concord Records (www.concordrecords.com). Among them: *Giant Strikes, Easy Street, Dancing in the Dark, A Handful of Stars, A Celebration of Hoagy Carmichael* and two volumes of *Dave McKenna Live at Maybeck Recital Hall,* a chapel-like room in the Berkeley hills.

On "Shadows and Dreams," John S. Wilson, for many years the chronicler of jazz nights for the New York Times, noted that Mr. McKenna "stretches out on a song by playing it in a variety of ways—for the sheer pleasure of the melody, then rumbling into a dark, swaggering but emphatically swinging attack that may burst into joyful stride piano before settling back to a gentle melodic caress."

The confident, ringing clarity of his sound conjures up Louis Armstrong. Although Mr. McKenna has absorbed much of jazz history, I also hear in his music echoes of the Harlem-based expansion of Eastern ragtime into the exuberant, two-handed, melodic liberation of the piano exemplified by Willie "The Lion" Smith, Luckey Roberts, James P. Johnson, Fats Waller, and Duke Ellington.

Just as saloons have become rare, so has this kind of playing. Someone once said of Smith: "When the Lion roared, you knew what was coming." But Mr. McKenna has not roared since January of last year. Living in a studio apartment in Providence, with a piano taking up much of the space, Mr. McKenna told me, "Diabetes got me bad. I have to walk with a cane. It's a severe neuropathy. And as for my hands, I have carpal tunnel syndrome." (Numbness, pain in the wrist, fingers, thumb, and palm.) He cannot play the piano.

Mr. McKenna says he never made any real money. As with many musicians, particularly the older players, royalties from recordings were never plentiful and often do not continue with reissues. Nonetheless, he says, "continuing tax hassles with the IRS are such that I wake up at two in the morning wondering when I'm going to be penniless."

Yet the spirit of his music is still stirring in him. "There's always hope. Maybe I haven't had my last gig. It's possible I'll play again. Thanks for remembering me."

Many people who have heard him play do remember him. In the notes for his *A Celebration of Hoagy*

Carmichael, Michael Bourne, a producer of jazz programs on WFIU-FM in Bloomington, Indiana, writes: "Once, after I'd played McKenna's solo Concord LPs on my radio program, someone rushed up to me on the street and kissed me.

"'What was that for?' I wondered, and she answered with a smile, 'Dave McKenna.' "

RALPH ELLISON:
LITERARY JAZZMAN

I t now seems inevitable that Ralph Waldo Ellison, growing up playing the trumpet in Oklahoma City— the home of jazz singer Jimmy Rushing and guitarist Charlie Christian, where blues singers Ma Rainey and Ida Cox performed—would someday write not only about being black in America (*Invisible Man*) but about jazz. And thanks to the vitality of his prose—along with his intimate understanding, from his Oklahoma city boyhood, of the social dynamics that shaped jazz's black originators—Ellison became the most evocative writer so far on "this American music."

There is no better introduction to the essence of jazz— and what Ellison (1914–1994) had to say about it—than *Living with Music: Ralph Ellison's Jazz Writings* (now available in paperback from Modern Library Classics). And some of the music that continually nourished his writing is on a Columbia/Legacy companion CD, *Living with Music: Ralph Ellison*, where lifelong influences Louis Armstrong, Bessie Smith, Duke Ellington, Jimmy Rushing, and Hot Lips Page can be found. From Armstrong's "Potato Head Blues," Ellington's "Black and Tan

Fantasy," Count Basie's "Moten Swing" and Billie Holiday's "All of Me," the music reverberates throughout Ellison's prose in the book. Abiding credit is due Robert O'Meally, the Columbia University professor of comparative literature who both edited the book and produced the CD.

Ellison's father, "raising this boy up to be a poet," named him after Ralph Waldo Emerson. The son, when later confronting segregation, decided: "If we are in a jug, it is transparent, not opaque, and one is allowed not only to see outside, but to read what is going on out there. So I read Marx, Freud, T. S. Eliot, Pound, Gertrude Stein, and Hemingway."

'Their Golden Horns'

In Oklahoma City, when he was fifteen, Ellison began to think of himself as a musician, playing gigs with small bands. Later, at Tuskegee Institute in Alabama, "I used to get up at five o'clock in the morning and play sustained tones out of the window just to learn to control an instrument, to develop tone."

Ellison eventually realized that he would never qualify to realize his ardent ambition to be in Duke Ellington's brass section. But what stayed with him, from boyhood on, was the impact of when "Ellington and the great orchestra came to town . . . with their uniforms, their skills, their golden horns, their flights of controlled and disciplined fantasy. . . .

"They were news from the great wide world, an example and a goal; and I wish that all those who write so knowledgeably of Negro boys having no masculine figures with whom to identify would consider the long national and international career of Ellington and his band, the thousands of one-night stands played in the black communities of this nation. Where in the white community, in any white community, could there have been found images, examples such as these? Who were so worldly, who so elegant, who so mockingly creative?"

On the *Living with Music* CD, Ralph Ellison's own voice is heard in an excerpt from his address at the Library of Congress in January 1964: "Long before I thought of writing, I was claimed by weather, by speech rhythms, by Negro voices and their different rhythms . . . by circuses and minstrel shows . . . by jazz musicians and fortune-tellers and by men who did anything well."

And because the jug of segregation allowed him to see outside, "'The Waste Land' seized my mind. I was intrigued by its power to move me while eluding my understanding. Somehow its rhythms were often closer to those of jazz than were those of the Negro poets; and even though I could not understand then, its range of allusion was as mixed and varied as that of Louis Armstrong."

Long before he found T. S. Eliot, Ellison heard Jimmy Rushing: "The voice was high and clear . . . possessed of a purity somehow impervious to both the stress of singing above a twelve-piece band and the urgency of Rushing's own blazing fervor . . . you could hear it jetting from the dance hall like a blue flame in the dark, now soaring high above the trumpets and trombones, now skimming the froth of reeds and rhythm as it called some woman's anguished name—or demanded in a high, thin, passionately lyrical line, 'Baaaaay-baby, Bay-aaay-bay! Tell me what's the matter now!'—above the shouting of the swinging band."

All-American

Ellison had little patience with Afrocentrism. In an interview with Mr. O'Meally, he said: "I've never identified with Africa. Now, I'm not denying my Afro-blood at all . . . [but] my strength comes from Louis Armstrong and Jimmy Rushing, Hot Lips Page, and people on that level, Duke Ellington . . . Mark Twain—all kinds of American figures who have been influenced by and contributed to that complex interaction of background and cultures which is specifically American."

And because of that complex interaction, he continued, "much of what's called white American culture wouldn't be what it is without us." Or, as he noted at the Library of Congress: "The small share of reality which each of our diverse groups is able to snatch from the whirling chaos of history belongs not to the group alone, but to all of us."

Remarkably, the first full-scale biography of Ellison— *Ralph Ellison: Emergence of Genius* by Lawrence Jackson of Howard University—was published only this year by John Wiley & Sons. Ellison's grandfather, Professor Jackson notes, was born a slave in South Carolina in 1837, one of "twenty-seven bondpeople . . . owned by widow Mary Ann Ellison."

Ellison's father, Lewis, who died when the boy was three years old, had been a soldier in the 25th U.S. Colored Infantry, the principal of a colored school, a construction worker, and a driver. He wanted his son to "not have to spend his life digging ditches or breaking stones." And he wished "that his son's life would not be as defined by race as was his own."

Firmly defining himself, Ellison found his own unmistakable voice as an American. When Mr. O'Meally was a student at Harvard, he approached Ellison, who was giving a talk, and asked: "Don't you think the Harlem Renaissance failed because we failed to create institutions to preserve our gains?"

Ellison looked at this young black man in a dashiki and said, "No." Then, Mr. O'Meally recalled, "just before being led toward the stage, he paused to look at me with steely eyes: 'We do have institutions. We have the Constitution and the Bill of Rights. And we have jazz.'"

CLIFFORD BROWN:
A TRUMPET AS SWEET
AS HIS SOUND

He made all of his recordings in the four years before he was killed in a car crash at the age of twenty-five in 1956. Benny Golson wrote a threnody, "I Remember Clifford," which was played so often by saddened musicians that it has become a standard. Players who were not alive in Clifford Brown's time speak of him reverentially.

And those who knew him, myself included, remember him not only as a dramatic, lyrical, and original trumpet player but also as a man utterly without malice or envy. In interviews, musicians (active forty years ago) characterize Clifford Brown as "sweet"—an attribute I've never heard applied to any other jazz musician. Brown, said Dizzy Gillespie, "wouldn't do anything that would remotely hurt your spirit. He was the only one of his kind. I loved him."

Brownie, as he was called, grew up in Wilmington, Delaware. His father played trumpet, violin, and piano for his own pleasure. "From the earliest time," Brownie once told me, "That trumpet fascinated me. When I was too little to reach it, I would climb up to where it was, and I kept knocking it down."

Sweet as he was, Brownie had a will of iron and subjected himself to vigorous discipline in his absorption in music. The music supervisor in the Wilmington Public Schools was Sam Wooding, who, in the 1920s, had been the first black jazz musician to tour Europe with a big band. He recalled that young Clifford Brown was "hungry to learn. You couldn't teach him fast enough." This delight in self-improvement lasted all the rest of his brief life. His widow, LaRue Brown Watson, says, "He used to practice all the time."

Working in Philadelphia, Clifford Brown soon gained a reputation for being able to get all around his horn—but with feeling. Charlie Parker heard him there and later, when Art Blakey was about to play a gig in Philadelphia, Parker told him: "Don't take a trumpet player. You won't need him after you hear Clifford Brown."

Brown, after a European tour with Lionel Hampton, went on to join Blakey, who played drums behind his soloists as if he were stoking a forest fire. Even in that combo, where Brown played swift sheets of notes, there was nearly always the thrust of a strong, joyful melodist with a passion for logic.

In 1954, the Clifford Brown–Max Roach quintet was formed, and during those last two years of Brown's life, he became so formidable a soloist that many musicians predicted he would become as pervasively influential as even Dizzy Gillespie. Also, when he became a co-leader, Brown, though no less gentle a friend and colleague, showed that he was unwilling to be taken advantage of by the middlemen of jazz. As Max Roach says, "He dealt with club owners and agents in no uncertain terms. He knew how to take care of himself."

And I remember that he—along with Quincy Jones, Donald Byrd, and a few other young jazzmen—wanted to learn a lot more about the business end of the music. How to find out, for example, what was really in the contracts they signed, including publishing contracts. (Brown's original compositions didn't just stay in the Brown-Roach repertory but were often adopted by other musicians.)

After a conversation with Clifford Brown—his soft-spoken speech as purposeful as his trumpet solos—I would hear him in a club. Undistracted by the noise of cash registers, waitresses, and customers enchanted with each other's conversations, Brown would raise his horn, and the impact of his music was what Thelonious Monk once described as a jazz musician's goal: "When you hit the bandstand, the bandstand is supposed to lift from the floor and the people are supposed to be lifted up too."

One can hear how Clifford Brown lifted up the listeners in a number of recently issued CDs. The most illuminating is *Brownie: The Complete EmArcy Recordings of Clifford Brown*, seven disks on the EmArcy label including sessions with Dinah Washington and Sarah Vaughn. There is also a one-volume *Clifford Brown and Max Roach* on Verve. And the earlier Brown has been collected in *Clifford Brown: The Complete Blue Note and Pacific*

Jazz Recordings on Blue Note/Pacific Jazz, manufactured by Capitol Records.

From standards played as if they were his own ("Stompin' at the Savoy," "You Go to My Head") to Clifford Brown originals ("Joy Spring," "Blues Walk"), there is a rejoicing in the improvising, in the continuous risk taking, in the stretching of the horn's possibilities and the stretching of what some jazz musicians call soul.

Like jazz players from before anybody used that word, Brown wanted to tell a story, a story that would keep the listener interested and a story the listener might remember after the music stopped. In a conversation I had with him in early 1955, Brown, speaking of the quintet he was leading with Max Roach, said: "Our own policy is to aim for the musical extremes of both excitement and subtle softness, whenever each is necessary, but with a lot of feeling in everything. We want to create emotional and intellectual tension."

After forty years, while some "modern jazz" of the 1940s and 1950s sounds like museum pieces, the player on these recordings continues to surprise, the deeply satisfying unpredictability of his life's work still energizing his singing horn.

SCOTT ROBINSON:
THE SOUND THAT TIME FORGOT

The C-melody saxophone is no longer manufactured, and it is in the arsenal of only a few contemporary jazzmen, among them Joe Lovano and Anthony Braxton. The only musician who features the horn is Scott Robinson, who was attracted to it when he was just starting because, he says, "it had a plaintive, yearning quality unique among saxophones—a sound full of hope, yet touched with a kind of loneliness and mystery. It became the sound that time forgot."

Mr. Robinson explores the lyrical, romantic scope of the instrument in the new *Scott Robinson Plays C-Melody Saxophone: Melody from the Sky*, on Arbors Records (800-299-1930). The company, based in Clearwater, Florida, is devoted to what it terms "classic jazz," but it carefully selects players who have their own, often surprising, stories to tell.

Scott Robinson disdains musical categories, having worked with Ruby Braff, Anthony Braxton, Toshiko Akiyoshi, Illinois Jacquet, Maria Schneider, and Buck Clayton. In each context, his playing—as critic Dan Morgenstern notes—"is idiomatically correct," but he doesn't sound like anyone else but himself. He has appeared on scores of recordings, mostly as a sideman, has received three fellowships from the National Endowment for the Arts, and has often played abroad. But he is not yet a "star"—except among musicians.

"Melody From the Sky" may help make his name more resounding. In multiple settings—duet with piano; organ trio; quintet including a trumpet; string quartet; quartet with an electric guitar—Mr. Robinson's ceaseless musical curiosity and imagination extend the emotional range of the C-melody saxophone beyond any of its previous appearances in jazz.

Characteristically, his repertory transcends categories. There are evocations of C-melody forebear Frankie Trumbauer, who played with Bix Beiderbecke ("Davenport Blues," "For No Reason at All in C," "Singin' the Blues"), as well as a rendition of Billy Strayhorn's haunting "Isfahan" and a moving, tender restoration of "Count Your Blessings," sung by Bing Crosby to Rosemary Clooney in the movie "White Christmas."

All the arrangements—each texturally, fondly specific to the diverse forms and moods—are by Mr. Robinson. Loren Schoenberg, who wrote the notes to this set, is himself a protean arranger and instrumentalist and has played with Mr. Robinson in many different contexts. He says of his frequent colleague that "music flows right out of him." That is manifest in his writing as well as his playing.

The legendary tenor saxophonist Lester Young, who had a conversational sound and graceful phrasing that influenced a larger school of international players, told me once in an interview that he himself had been deeply influenced by Frankie Trumbauer, a white musician.

"He was my idol," Young said. "When I had just started to play, I used to buy all his records. He played the C-melody saxophone, and I tried to get that sound on tenor. That's why I don't sound like other people. Nobody played like Trumbauer. That's what knocked me out."

When listening to a player with prodigious technique, Young would say, "Well, what's your story? What are you saying?" And Young so liked Trumbauer, he would say, because of the stories he told. Scott Robinson speaks too, through his horn, of memories, desires, and illuminations that can't be put into words; his solo in "Singin' the Blues" sounds so private that I had the feeling I was eavesdropping.

There is another dimension to Mr. Robinson, evident in his 1997 Arbors release "Thinking Big," in which he plays clarinet and bass clarinet; C-melody, alto, tenor, baritone, soprano, bass, and contrabass saxophones; theremin; and contrabass sarrusophone. Ordinarily, so profligate a multi-instrumentalist appears to be—and sounds like—a novelty act, like in old-time vaudeville. But Mr. Robinson, as natural and personal on each of them as he is on the C-melody saxophone, keeps telling stories in different colors.

As in "Melody from the Sky," the choice of songs reflects his omnivorous knowledge and curiosity about the mosaic of jazz. He is, for example, an admirer of the utterly uncategorizable Sun Ra ("Dreams Come True"), who claimed to have come to Earth as a bearer of good will from another planet. There are also tributes to Duke Ellington ("Mood Indigo," "All Too Soon," "On a Turquoise Cloud"); but they're in Mr. Robinson's distinctive language, which, in his arrangement of "Mood Indigo," includes the eerily penetrating sound of the theremin—an electronic instrument that is played by passing one's hands over a small black box.

Years ago, during my time in radio, an elderly man who seemed to almost levitate played the theremin every Sunday morning during a theosophical program. I often wondered what was in that black box, but was not eager to find out. Here, the theremin makes "Mood Indigo" sound as if it were being played in a fathomless dream.

Mr. Robinson also found a Lil Hardin Armstrong song, "My Heart," that the pianist and then-wife of Louis Armstrong composed for one of the legendary Hot Five sessions. And he surprised me by including "Chances Are," which he learned from working with Johnny Mathis, who made it a hit. But Mr. Robinson on tenor, backed only by Bucky Pizzarelli on seven-string guitar, is more elegantly intimate than the pop singer.

An index of the breadth of Mr. Robinson's engagements is that he has performed in more than a dozen countries in a single year; has spoken at a Congressional Black Caucus Jazz Forum; and has conducted jazz workshops, arranged by the U.S. Embassy, in the Czech Republic.

The C-melody saxophone is no longer the sound that time forgot.

Ruby Braff:
Horn Player Ruby Braff
Was Anything But Old-Fashioned

At fourteen, playing clarinet before an open window at my home in Boston, fantasizing about one day sitting in Duke Ellington's reed section, I heard a gruff shout from a short kid on the sidewalk: "You want to go to a session?" I hurried along, figuring I could read any arrangement although I didn't know how to improvise. As soon as I heard the kid, the impatient twelve-year-old Ruby Braff, creating singing melodies on his trumpet, I knew I'd better start thinking about a day job. He was jazz itself.

Three years later, already a pro, Ruby was working at Izzy Ort's, a dive next to the RKO Theater where the big jazz bands were often booked. Walking out of the stage door one night, Benny Goodman was drawn into Izzy Ort's by the sound of a horn played by Ruby, standing on a box behind the piano to hide his age. Goodman wanted to take him on the road, but Ruby's mother wouldn't hear of it. The kid had to finish high school.

Born in Boston in 1927, her son immersed himself in jazz from the time he was six, especially in the endless surprises of Louis Armstrong. "This beautiful, bright orange sound came out of the radio," he often recalled, "and I was in the Louis Armstrong University, from which you never graduate."

In 1956, Armstrong voted for Ruby Braff in the "New Star" category of the Encyclopedia of Jazz Yearbook poll. By then, Mr. Braff was playing the more intimate cornet, and it was Armstrong who told him to stop using mutes: "What do you want to use those things for? Play with your own sound."

In Boston, and then in New York, Ruby gained the respect of such classic-jazz originals as Pee Wee Russell, Buck Clayton, Vic Dickenson, Edmond Hall, and Ellis Larkins, before leading his own groups. When he met Charlie Parker, Ruby was surprised that this icon of modern jazz said he liked his playing. "I thought he was putting me on," Ruby told me, "until I found out as we talked that he liked the same things in music I did. He was very close to the blues and had beautiful melodic conception."

Ruby's credo: "I believe in beauty, music that takes people to a delicious place that they can't ordinarily get to in their own lives." As for his sound, he said, "It looks as if I'm playing a cornet, but when I'm playing, I'm really thinking of a cello. Most people play three times louder than they should. Music should be played at a conversational level."

The English critic Steve Voce said of Ruby: "Unimpressed by high notes for their own sake, he opened up new depth in the bottom registers of the instrument that others could not reach." Off the stand, Mr. Braff was as independent as his music. He did not suffer fools—and most other people—gladly. And because he would not compromise his music as fashions in jazz changed, he never made much money.

But over time, in this country, and particularly in England, he acquired and held a growing audience. And he appeared on more than 200 LPs and CDs. Shortly before he died of emphysema and other ailments at a nursing home in North Chatham, Massachusetts, on February 9, 2003, he told his sister, Susan Atran, that he regretted not having married and had children. He never thought he had enough financial security to start a family. "Our family name will die," he said.

"Ruby," his sister told him, "you reached so many people with your music, and you made so many records, your name will live forever. How many other people could say that?"

Starting in 1993, he made many of the recordings that most satisfied him for Arbors Records (800-299-1930), a classic-jazz label owned by Matt Domber. "I've recorded for I can't count how many labels, some here, some abroad," Ruby told Charles Champlin of the *Los Angeles Times*, "and Matt Domber gives me more freedom than I've ever had before."

Also enduring are *Ruby Braff and Ellis Larkins: The Grand Reunion* and *Ruby and Woody Herman: It Had to Be Us,* both on Chiaroscuro. Of the Arbors sets, *Being with You: Ruby Braff Remembers Louis Armstrong* reminds me of a story that Mr. Braff's friend Jack Brad-ley, who was also a friend of Armstrong, tells of when Ruby was in a coma in the mid-1900s at Cape Cod Hospital.

For days, Ruby had not responded to anything. Mr. Bradley brought to his room a cassette player and a tape of Armstrong singing "I'm in the Mood for Love." It was a 1938 recording, not his more renowned 1936 version of the song. Mr. Bradley recalls: "About ten seconds after Pops began singing, Ruby slowly opened his eyes. I could actually see the color returning to his face as he shook his head. 'That's a different take,' Ruby said, and a few min-utes later, fully awake, Ruby added, 'That's the second time Pops has saved my life.' "

"When was the first?" Jack Bradley asked. "The first time I heard him," Ruby answered.

Like Louis Armstrong's, Ruby Braff's music will never date. As Mr. Champlin wrote, his "style is so personal, distinctive and instantly recognizable that it can only evoke Ruby Braff himself."

Yet, the February 11 headline on his *New York Times* obituary was: "Ruby Braff, an Old-style Trumpeter and Cornetist, 75." And the lead paragraph described him as having "defied the odds by rising to fame in the modern era with a resolutely old-fashioned style." I can well imag-ine Ruby's response in language that, as used to be said, would not be fit for a family newspaper.

The day that obituary appeared, I was talking to Jim Hall, the world-class jazz guitarist, who shook his head in exasperation at what he had also read in the *Times*. "Ruby has his own voice," Mr. Hall said. "There's nothing old-fashioned about playing beautifully like that."

In his last days, Ruby received messages from listeners in other countries, and frequent calls from Tony Bennett, for whom he was a soloist from 1971 to 1973. Bennett is no more "old-style" than Ruby Braff. Ruby's mother used to say of her singular son, "We don't know where we got him." Louis Armstrong knew.

AGELESS BIG
AND SMALL BANDS

JAZZ FOR LUNCH
AT THE CAJUN

L ong ago, Whitney Balliett described jazz as "the sound of surprise." That continual proof of the music's life force seized me once again listening to Stefon Harris' *The Grand Unification Theory* (Blue Note)—a wondrous mosaic of freshly multicolored writing with intriguingly subtle dynamics, along with singular soloists. His music needs no labels like "postmodern" or "cutting edge." It is Stefon Harris music, as Charles Mingus', he insisted, was Mingus music.

At lunch recently at the Cajun, a restaurant on Eighth Avenue and 16th Street in New York, where you can get Louisiana catfish, I was surprised at how much pleasure there still is in some of the jazz I grew up with. Many years ago, at Lester Young's then home in Queens, after a long interview, I was almost out the door when he, the embodiment of what was "hip" in jazz at the time (off as well as on the bandstand), said to me: "Do you like Dixieland?"

"Sure," I answered, "if it's good."

"Me too," said Pres.

Every Wednesday, from 12:30 to 2 PM at the Cajun, what the Gotham Jazzmen play for those who need labels, is not strictly Dixieland, though the repertory includes "Hello, Central, Give Me Doctor Jazz," and "The Original Dixieland One Step." But there's also a lot of Gershwin and Jerome Kern. The beat, and therefore the soloists, move in the swing-rhythm waves that characterized Eddie Condon's crews ("Nicksieland") and the good-time music of Jimmy McPartland and the Bob Crosby Bob Cats. The band, with the same name and somewhat overlapping personnel, has also been playing since 1976 on Thursdays from 12:30 to 2 PM, at the public Donnell Library in Manhattan. No admission charge. Trombonist Jim Collier, who played with Max Kaminsky and Wild Bill Davison, among others, says: "We never rehearse, rarely take requests, and have never tried to promote the band. We frequently play tunes we don't know very well—or don't know at all—partly because of professionals, semipros, and amateurs.

"Most of us," Collier continues, "have played in fairly fast company on occasion and some of us still do. I think nearly everyone in the band played at the old 54th Street Condon's and Jimmy Ryan's on 52nd Street at some time." Some of the names may be known to readers of *JazzTimes*: trumpeter Peter Ecklund, who has four CDs under his own name; guitarist Dawes Thompson, who worked with Milt Hinton and Vic Dickenson, among others; and pianist Peter Sokolow, a practicing expert in what Fats Waller and James P. Johnson made of stride piano, as well as having toured Europe several times with Klezmer bands. A mixed bag of musicians, some with day jobs who don't care about critics' categories or polls so long as they can get together and play.

The Gotham Jazzmen will surely never be part of National Public Radio's (NPR) dwindling jazz programming, but I bet there are many listeners around the country who either, as I did, were hooked for life as kids on this kind of music that made you feel so good—or would be if exposed. For listeners like me, as Al Cohn told me as we were leaving the Great South Bay Jazz Festival that had featured a reunion of survivors of the Fletcher Henderson band (Gerry Mulligan, naturally, sat in): "You never lose a feeling for the music that first for you involved in jazz." After all, as Lester Young said to me that afternoon in Queens, it was Frank Trumbauer who turned him on early ("He always told a little story").

In a letter in the June *JazzTimes* ("Hentoff Wrong") by Murray Horwitz, former vice president of NPR's cultural programming, he admits that NPR has "largely abdicated its leadership role in [jazz] programming," but, he says, the blame is on the NPR stations in the largest markets that are driven "almost entirely on audience ratings." But the national NPR audience had risen from more 13 million in 1998 to nearly 20 million last fall. So, if the national NPR programmers are interested in sizable, durable audiences for jazz, they should look at any issue of the monthly *Mississippi Rag*, which has extensive listings of locations around the country that include many clubs booking music much like that played by the Gotham Jazzmen.

The Cajun is there, along with such clubs as Ruga's in Oakland, New Jersey, and the City Saloon in Columbia, Illinois. In most of these clubs, the sessions aren't every night, and some not every week. But others, like the Cajun, have such combos on different nights during the week as Vince Giordano's Nighthawks, the Red Onion Jazz Band, and the Canal Street Dixieland & Blues Band. If Frank Trumbauer were alive, he would be playing at one of those clubs. And the long list of jazz festivals across the nation in the *Mississippi Rag* has a large proportion of bands in the long-distance tradition of the Gotham Jazzmen.

Not only listeners who were drawn to these sounds as youngsters dig this music these days. When more or less traditional jazz groups play in schools, these kids can't help dancing. Not only NPR, but also much of the established jazz network—record companies, magazines, book publishers, public and commercial television—ignore these musicians and their fans. But the bands, like the Gotham Jazzmen, keep on for the sheer pleasure of the ride.

Jubilant Sounds Swinging
Through America

Just as our Constitution—as Justice John Marshall said—is a living document, not fixed in the time of its origin, so too the free spirit of jazz keeps changing as it moves on. But largely lost have been the big jazz bands that for years filled the nation's ballrooms and those clubs big enough to hold them.

As a boy growing up during the big-band era, I likened those exultant ensembles to the flare of trains roaring through the American night. Swinging through towns and cities from coast to coast, these crisp musicians lighted the dark with excitement, surprises, and romance. An enduring memory is standing as close as I could get to the magisterial Duke Ellington orchestra in a Boston ballroom, and whispering to baritone saxophonist Harry Carney at the end of a number, "What was the name of that?"

"He hasn't named it yet," was the genial answer. I had heard history in the making.

There are still some traveling big bands, but none with the luster of Ellington, Count Basie, Jimmie Lunceford, and Andy Kirk & His Clouds of Joy, among many others.

These bands are among the twenty joyful orchestras in the three-CD set *Big Band Jazz/The Jubilee Sessions/ 1943–1946* (Hindsight Records, available from that cornucopia of invaluable reissues, Mosaic Records, 203-327-7111, www.mosaicrecords.com).

Peter Kline, who assembled these sessions for Hindsight, tells me that most of the performances were actual live recordings of airchecks, along with a few rehearsals and some studio tracks. They were originally cut by Armed Forces Radio and aired primarily for black service personnel during the war years. Hindsight, formed by the late Wally Heider, has never gone in much for promotion, so I didn't know about this treasure trove until the label's Don Mupo sent it to this fellow big-band enthusiast.

In addition to the aforementioned renowned bands, there are jubilant sounds from the battalions of Lucky Millinder, Benny Carter, Earl "Fatha" Hines (one of the hottest of the big bands), Erskine Hawkins, Billy Eckstine (where many later icons of modern jazz were sidemen), and the International Sweethearts of Rhythm, who proved that men have no monopoly on swinging and unmistakably individual soloist sounds. Listening to such "Sweethearts" as tenor saxophonist Viola Burnside would not reveal the gender of the player as the horn bursts into "Tuxedo Junction" and the rhythm section comes on like the Wabash Cannonball locomotive.

Coursing through all the Jubilee sessions is the musicians' sheer collective delight in being part of this glorious American enterprise that so entranced the home-folks across the land. Ralph Ellison remembered the impact of the bands on him as a boy in *Living with Music* (the Modern Library):

"Their uniforms, their sophistication, their skills, their golden horns, their flights of controlled and disciplined fantasy. . . . They were news from the great wide world."

Among the timeless skills of the players on these tracks is the soulful, worldly-wise singing of Jimmy Rushing, found here in "I'm Gonna Move to the Outskirts of Town" at a 1943 Count Basie rehearsal. And the golden tenor horn of often forgotten Paul Bascomb on "The Bear Mash Blues" reminded me of the deeply satisfying consistency of the Erskine Hawkins orchestra, which deserves much more attention in jazz histories and reissue projects.

I had entirely forgotten the arranging and composing mastery of Jimmy Mundy, who scored "Sing, Sing, Sing" and "Swingtime in the Rockies" for Benny Goodman and "Queer Street" for Count Basie. Leading his own band on several shows in this set, Mundy's easy rolling "Hello, Goodbye, Forget" exemplifies what "grooving" means.

On the Andy Kirk and his Clouds of Joy sessions, the disciplined passion of the long overlooked trumpet player Howard McGhee is showcased on "McGhee Special." Also seldom mentioned in jazz magazines these days is the distinctive, often rollicking, Jimmie Lunceford Harlem Express, which combined precise showmanship with adventurous solos and unexpected ensemble voicings.

The opening of the sensuous Lunceford version of "Alone Together" recalled Duke Ellington telling me of how when alto saxophonist Johnny Hodges was playing a ballad at a dance and a sigh came from the floor, "that sigh became part of our music." That relationship between the dancer-listener and the jazz storyteller was long at the core of the jazz experience, but is found mostly these nights in memories.

While Earl Hines is remembered primarily for his "trumpet-style" piano and his early recordings with Louis Armstrong, his big band—as in "Scoops Carry Mary," recorded at a show in Hollywood in 1944—has such energizing drive that back then I'd put his recordings on when I wanted a special lift.

As Tom Reed recalls in the notes to the Jubilee Sessions, in those years, "There was no Civil Rights Act, no integration to speak of, and yet it was a period of supreme African American artistry under conditions of duress. . . . As these great bands traveled from coast to coast, they encountered the 'Colored can't stay—but they can play' signs with regard to hotel accommodations. White night clubs featured African American bands for White Clientele only—and there were 'we serve colored in the rear' signs when it came to finding a place to eat, as they toured from town to town."

But, as Ralph Ellison wrote, "Who were so worldly, who so elegant, who so mockingly creative? . . . And who treated the social limitations placed in their paths with greater disdain?" But also with no little anger, as I heard sidemen tell of Jim Crow waiting outside the ballroom or the stage door.

All of it—the pride, the anger, the anticipation of making more joy in the next set—is in the music, thanks to Armed Forces Radio and Hindsight, which has an extensive catalog of rare big- and small-combo jazz of all colors, available at 800-775-8467.

A Thrilling
Big Jazz Band

George Wein and I were trying recently to find the right word to describe the rush of excitement that hits you when a player or a band is really cooking (a term from our youth). We settled on "thrilling." For me, it was hearing a Lee Morgan cadenza on "Night in Tunisia" in a band that Dizzy Gillespie himself was leading, or Sonny Stitt immobilizing diners and waiters at New York's Basin Street East with a stop-time chorus.

I get that thrill from a big band, Diva, which has played prestigious festivals in Europe—and in the States hits some towns so small that the prestige restaurant is a Pizza Hut. Because the band doesn't get enough consecutive gigs in a year—maybe 30 to 35 altogether—the side-women freelance, play in Broadway shows and teach. But the center of their musical lives is the band. Diva's drummer-leader is Sherrie Maricle, whose day job is director of percussion studies at New York University, where she has twice been voted teacher of the year. As a composer-arranger, she transcends categories.

None of the established jazz record labels has room these days for Diva, so its new release, *Live in Concert:*

Sherrie Maricle and the Diva Jazz Orchestra, is self-produced. (You can buy it at Diva's Web site, diva-jazz.com.) The performance was recorded at the Manchester Craftsmen's Guild in Pittsburgh on June 21, 2002. From note one, the powerful swinging pulse of the band made me wish I still had a jazz-radio program, as I used to in Boston and New York. I would set up a blindfold test for every guest musician and put on a track or two from this Diva set. I would bet my rare International Sweethearts of Rhythm recording that no one would be able to identify the gender of the players.

Diva began in 1992, cofounded by Maricle, John LaBarbara and Stanley Kay, the creative director. Kay is the band's manager and tireless cheerleader. A former drummer, he managed Buddy Rich and Gregory and Maurice Hines. As for Diva, he advises one and all, "Turn around and tell me if women or men are playing." From the blazing opener, Kay's "Did You Do That?" to Deborah Weisz's subtle conversational trombone during "In a Mellotone" and Lisa Parrott's robust, thrusting baritone saxophone on "I've Got the World on a String," Diva's infectious spirit and exultant cohesiveness are what drew me into jazz when I was 11 years old. I was struck on the street, as if by lightning, by Artie Shaw's "Nightmare" coming from a record store.

Max Roach and Martin Williams used to liken jazz to the essence of democracy—self-expression further energized and magnified in active collaboration with one's peers. In jazz, this often-joyous intersection is amplified in a big band. When Diva played Croatia, they received 15 bouquets at the end of the performance—a tribute hardly likely for an all-male band. But what comes through consistently and persistently in Diva's music is not exotica—chicks with chops!—but the very essence of the jazz experience. Miles Davis and I were once talking about some critics and listeners who divide music, any kind of music, into categories. "Andre Watts," Miles said, "plays a good piano; so does Bill Evans. Everyone who's out there is connected, not pigeonholed according to some label."

Including pigeonholed by gender. That Diva doesn't get more gigs, particularly in the U.S., where jazz began, is due in part to the limited attention it gets in the jazz press. And that comes, I believe, from the continuing assumption, however subliminal, that women singers and pianists can be admitted to the fraternity; but women instrumentalists, let alone all-female bands, still have to prove that they have the "balls" to be authentic jazzmakers. Oh, there are interesting features, sometimes sections, in jazz magazines on women in jazz, but the attitude is often that of noblesse oblige, like making sure there are enough blacks on television sitcoms.

Here is Diva—not a pickup band for record dates, still out there on a bus, along with the other doughty surviving big bands, and with a signature sound and distinctive soloists, getting standing ovations on most of its gigs. Yet in *Down Beat's* big band issue this year, there was no mention of Diva, nor was Diva to be found in the Women in Jazz issue of *Jazziz*. But in the band's promotional material, there is an earlier citation from *Jazz times*: "The band punched, kicked, roared and swung with a disciplined abandon and unaffected joie de vivre." And in the British magazine *Crescendo* Geoff Burdett writes of the *Live in Concert* CD: "I confess to being very surprised by the sheer power and spirit of this band, quite apart from the very high level of musical ability on display. . . . Make no mistake, these girls can play, and I mean play."

If there were still big band cutting sessions, "these girls" would swing a lot of the remaining big bands out of the place. And maybe that news would bring them the attention in the jazz press and elsewhere that they deserve. I hope this column will bring them more radio play. But what I often did on the air was not announce the names until after the recording. That would startle some macho listeners.

THE BUSINESS OF JAZZ

JOHN LEVY:
A PERSONAL MANAGER
BEYOND CATEGORY

I n a 1961 piece, the British jazz critic and historian
Albert McCarthy quoted from a letter sent him by a
jazz musician: "Jazz is not just an art remote from life.
It's a matter of going out in the street and making a living . . . and the street is often a dirty place."

That same year, in the July issue of *Metronome*, I used
that quote in a column about how hard it was for jazz
musicians to find someone who knew the business to
guide them through the minefields on the street.

"Honest personal managers with stamina, confidence
and knowledge," I noted, "are exceedingly hard to find.
John Levy, one of the very best, has almost more clients
than he can handle."

I first knew John as a bass player with, among many
others, Stuff Smith, Billie Holiday, and George Shearing.
He thought of himself "as a good journeyman bassist,"
but not a soloist. Yet Duke Ellington asked him to join the
orchestra, but John turned him down because the money

wasn't that good and 52nd Street, where he was working, was much too exciting to leave.

When John became George Shearing's full-scale personal manager—not just an agent—he was one of the first personal jazz managers in the business. And he was the first major league black personal manager. Through the years, his clients—many of whom became close friends—included Nat and Cannonball Adderley, Joe Williams, Nancy Wilson, and Wes Montgomery.

At eighty-nine, still spruce and active, John has written the most revealing inside book so far on what is often "the dirty place" that is the business of jazz. Some of the lists of clubs, dates, and trips could have been shortened, but with his chronic honesty, John has added significantly to the largely neglected history of what it takes to make a living in jazz.

Men, Women and Girl Singers: My Life As a Musician Turned Talent Manager is published by the Beckham Publication Group (phone 301-384-7995 or www.beckhamhouse.com). It was written with Devra Hall, a longtime business associate of John's and now his companion. She is the daughter of guitarist Jim Hall.

I don't have the space to go into the stories about the off-stand lives, reverses, and resilience of the many musicians John chronicles. But to give a sense of his unsparing look at the predators on the business end, he writes of Birdland in its glory days: "It was really gangster dominated. You could always see these thugs sitting around in there, so you knew."

I was a regular at Birdland, and one night, I saw a familiar big-time living mug shot. A waiter identified him as a prominent member of what millions now see in *The Sopranos*. He was not at Birdland to dig Count Basie.

Of particular value in the book, however, is what it tells of how pervasive Jim Crow was in the music business. Not only on the road for black players, and managers, but in the record companies.

During the 1950s, when John signed George Shearing to Capitol Records, John said to Nat Cole, who was doing a session with George Shearing: "The only black person in this entire company is the janitor." By the early 1970s, John writes, "Arnold Larkin was the first black man to be on the legal staff at Capitol, and he knew where the bodies were buried and how much the different artists were making. This time around we doubled the amount of Nancy Wilson's advance."

In 1976, negotiating a deal for another artist with Warner Brothers Records, a lawyer John consulted about the contract told him: "This is the black deal." As John explains: "The recording industry used two separate types of contracts: one that they offered to white artists and another that was used for black artists. The royalty rates were usually lower, the advance was always lower and the amount of money they put into promotion was always lower in the black contracts. Except for the black superstars—they get a very good budget. . . . And sadly, I don't believe that separate black arrangements have really changed that much."

The book also points out that the first black executive at a record company was Quincy Jones—as late as 1961.

Quincy wrote the introduction to *Men, Women and Girl Singers*. He says the book "is especially important for aspiring young blacks, who in a lot of cases have had no exposure to the history of the people or personalities that have made it possible for them to be able to perform or to follow their craft."

With so many colleges now offering courses in the history of jazz, surely some scholar with an MBA degree may finally do a comprehensive history of the business end of jazz.

Art Davis:
The Mystery of Making It

Coleman Hawkins used to tell of a young player he heard in the Midwest. "He had it," Bean said, "but I told him, 'You'll never make it unless you get to New York.'" Hawkins never mentioned him again, and all these years later, I've forgotten the musician's name. I expect like a number of truly inventive local and regional players who have remained unknown outside their territory, that tenor player stayed where he was, for whatever reasons.

But Art Davis, a bassist with a stunning command of his instrument, who made any kind of a gig—from Louis Armstrong and Dizzy Gillespie to James Brown and Minnie Pearl—did make it on the New York jazz scene. He was John Coltrane's favorite bassist and Charles Mingus had the same highest regard for his sound, time and a voice that was authoritatively his own.

But because, as players back then used to say, Davis had "big ears," he could fuse that voice into just about any mosaic without losing it. I remember those Coltrane numbers that could last for well over an hour with, as

Davis recalls, "people shouting, just like in a holy-roller church" and Davis stretching out as far as Coltrane.

Art Davis, off the stand, also made himself heard. As brilliantly at ease in classical music as in jazz, he applied and was denied a place in symphony orchestras. As I wrote, at the time, in an article for the now defunct magazine, *The Reporter*, black musicians were frozen out of those jobs, partly because Jim Crow was in the wings but also because of favoritism. First chair players especially—all of whom were white—would push their very best students—all of whom were white—into some of the positions as they opened.

Art, in interviews with me, among others, would challenge symphony orchestras to pit him against any classical bassist of their choice. There was no response. He kept speaking and writing about this form of exclusion—including the steep hurdles for women in those orchestras and now feels that he lost a good many gigs in other fields because he was targeted as a troublemaker.

After scuffling for some ten years in New York, Art moved on to California where he teaches part time at the University of California at Irvine, Orange Coast College, and Goldenwest in Orange County. He also gives private lessons for advanced students and for professionals who feel the need to be challenged.

Based in Long Beach, he works around town and visits schools of all grades to spread the gospel of jazz, as Art Blakey used to. He also has a nonprofit organization, Better Advantages for Students and Society (B.A.S.S.), that awards scholarships to students, in and out of music, who keep growing but need the extra bread.

In terms of the national scene, Davis has slipped out of sight. Recently, I spoke about John Coltrane at the annual John Coltrane tribute and concert at Northeastern University in Boston. Some of the musicians were talking about Art Davis and wondered what he was doing now. None of the jazz labels has asked him to head a session as a leader and instrumentalist or as a composer. To the older players I spoke to, Art was sort of a vanished legend.

Not surprisingly, however—in view of the history of advanced jazz appreciation in other climes—Art Davis still has a considerable following in Germany and Japan. And not long ago, he toured Europe with David Murray's All-Stars. Murray, himself notably outspoken, has said: "A lot of people have lost the idea of having a signature sound. Still, when you get to be about thirty or thirty-five years old, you should be developing into your own sound, but now they've gone for excessive notes."

David Murray knows a signature sound when he hears one. In Edward Berger's book, *Bassically Speaking* (Scarecrow Press) about George Duvivier (as magisterial a presence off as well as on the stand), Duvivier says of Coleman Hawkins, who gave him his first important gig: "Hawk never stopped listening. . . . You never knew what would come out. It was almost unnerving how intently he could listen."

That's how I used to feel watching and listening to Art Davis during those Coltrane nights when time stopped, except for jazz time. Davis is far from idle, but he says, "My abilities have still not yet been fully challenged." That reminded me of what Jimmy Rowles said when I asked him what he did between gigs. "I listen for the phone to ring," said Jimmy.

Art Davis can be reached at 562-621-9614.

MUSICIANS TAKING
CARE OF THEIR OWN

At the double-feature movies when I was a kid, there often was an intermission during which someone would stand up and ask for contributions to the Will Rogers home for impoverished actors who needed a place to stay and, frequently, medical help.

Forty years ago, when I was covering the jazz scene full-time, I had a fantasy of a similar place for jazz musicians who had fallen on hard times and who needed such fundamentals of survival as rent money and free hospitalization because most of them, being essentially free-lancers, had no medical benefits. That's not a fantasy any more. Starting in 1989, and continually expanding its services, The Jazz Foundation of America (JFA)—and its Jazz Musicians' Emergency Fund—has helped hundreds of musicians renew and strengthen their lives.

In a remarkable act of commitment to jazz players who fall ill, the Englewood Hospital in New Jersey, in connection with The Jazz Foundation, provides free—I emphasize free—medical care. It was at that hospital that Dizzy Gillespie died, and it was his extraordinary energizing warmth and spirit that helped this hospital—and its Dr. Francis Forte, chief of oncology and an amateur jazz musician—to memorialize Dizzy in a way that would have given him great satisfaction. There is a Dizzy Gillespie Cancer Institute at the hospital. So far, one of the treatments at Englewood would have cost a musician $60,000—and there is still no limit on the number of musicians who will be treated for free.

Meanwhile, in association with The Jazz Foundation, a hospital in Manhattan is planning a program in preventive medicine for jazz performers.

To quality for the free medical care and hospitalization at Englewood, a musician must have been in the music business full-time for ten years or more and be without health insurance or be underinsured for the particular problem that needs attention. The Jazz Foundation points out that up to this point in time, more than 150 jazz artists have been treated for such conditions as quadruple bypass surgery, and provided chemotherapy, as well as two hip replacement operations.

There is nothing comparable in the United States—or anywhere in the world—to the range and depth of services that The Jazz Foundation provides. Anyone anywhere who is turned to the life force that is jazz can belong to The Jazz Foundation. Levels of tax deductible membership begin at $30 and the address is 322 W. 48th Street, New York, NY 10036. Telephone: 212-245-3999 or 1-800-532-5267.

Trumpeter Jimmy Owens and bassist Jamil Nasser were among the initial organizers of the foundation and remain very active officers of the organization. The president is Herb Storfer, who formerly was the jazz archivist at the Schomburg library in Harlem, a vital center of information about all dimensions of black history and culture. The executive director of the foundation is Monet Molock, who has a theater background.

In finding out about the foundation, I finally discovered what happened to Phineas Newborn—a pianist of phenomenal techniques and singular conception. Years ago, I listened and watched with wonder at one of his recording sessions. Phineas' unnecessarily grim final chorus is described in a brochure for the Jazz Musicians' Emergency Fund: "His body lies in a pauper's grave in Memphis due to a lack of funds for a proper burial." There have been many other musicians whose lives would have been regenerated if enough of us cared.

Recently, at the Blue Note in New York, Clark Terry— the very model of the buoyant life force that is jazz— received the foundation's newest Lifetime Achievement Award. The evening's proceeds went to the foundation. Singing that night—with grace and power—was Teri Thornton, who told how the foundation changed her life.

After hours of listening to jazz soul music that night, I left thinking of what Jo Jones once told me of what it was like in Kansas City when there was jazz around the clock. "People would go from club to club," Jo said, "walking in jazz time." That's how I walked home that night, lifted by seeing and hearing all those musicians and their admirers taking care of their own.

MUSICIANS IN NEED

The concert on September 24 for and by the Jazz Foundation of America (JFA) at Harlem's Apollo Theater raised money for rent, car repairs, medical prescriptions, and other necessities for musicians in need. But the week after the concert, Wendy Oxenhorn, the Foundation's executive director, wrote: "Before the concert, we were assisting twice as many musicians as we had ever helped, about six to eight musicians a day. This week, I found I'm working on ten cases before 2 PM, and by night's end, I add a few more."

It's not only in New York and surrounding cities that there are jazz musicians out of work and out of luck. In the March 5 *New York Times*, Rick Bragg told of musicians in similar straits in New Orleans: "The outside world—the world of rent checks and health insurance and retirement plans—is for other people, not musicians." New Orleans singer-pianist-songwriter-producer Allen Toussaint added, "It can happen to so many people"— including musicians listed on jazz reissue recordings, who keep clips from old mentions in jazz magazines. Oxenhorn notes that a musician who is on one of the reissue CDs released in connection with Ken Burns' *Jazz* series "came into our offices and was unable to pay for his $150 diabetes medication."

In his report from New Orleans, Rick Bragg told of a monument in a paupers field there to Charles "Buddy" Bolden, who was already a legend when guitarist Danny Barker was coming up in New Orleans. "When he played that horn," Danny told me, "you could hear him for blocks." The monument reads: "In an unmarked grave near here rests Buddy Bolden. Legendary cornet player, New Orleans jazz pioneer. And first 'King of Jazz.'" But the grave is still unmarked. As Bragg writes, "His body is said to have been moved so many times to make room for other plots that caretakers lost it." I wonder how many other jazz musicians, listed in discographies in many languages, wound up in paupers fields.

Back in New York, Oxenhorn is working on a new project for the Jazz Foundation. "Half of the battles that the JFA fights," she writes, "are eviction-related because many of the elderly musicians live in rent-controlled apartments that landlords could rent for more money." Landlords are trying to evict their tenants at every chance. "Many of the musicians we assist," she continues, "do not make enough to pay their rent or are behind in their rent, because they are not able to play as many gigs as they did when they were younger because illness and ailments slow them down."

And for many, the gigs have disappeared. The phone doesn't ring anymore. She makes another very important point that many devoted listeners to the music don't have in mind as they enjoy the continuing treasures of reissues: "The older musicians also have financial problems and do not have savings because they were never paid properly for their work. They were always paid in cash and never received pension plans. Even when they did record, they did not have royalties as an option. When LPs are reissued to CDs, the musicians usually do not receive any money. All they ever received was a one-time buyout. In most cases, this still holds true for today's musicians."

I would appreciate hearing from musicians whose recordings from years ago are now out again. Are they receiving any royalties? Write to me in care of *JazzTimes*.

Oxenhorn's new project is a Players Residence in New York City. "Housing," she emphasizes, "is not affordable for the aging jazz musician. The musicians that are lucky enough to receive social security, get about $500 a month at most. It's almost impossible to find even a room for rent that is below $600 a month in New York City." The Jazz Foundation is trying to renovate a building that will be a home for elder jazz musicians, with "studio apartments for $250 a month, so that even the most meager income or social security check would pay the rent. This would allow the older jazz musicians to live on the few gigs they get each month. No one in the history of jazz has built a home in honor of the musicians."

I'll keep you informed as these plans for a players residence materializes. To become a member of the Jazz Foundation of America, you can send a tax-deductible contribution to: Jazz Foundation of America, 322 W. 48th Street, New York, NY 10036 (phone: 212-245-3999 or 1-800-532-5267). Record companies and jazz clubs should add to what they've already given—if they've contributed at all. Remember Buddy Bolden.

When Dizzy Liberated Himself

When I came to New York in 1953 to run the *Down Beat* office there, I spent just about all of my time with jazz musicians. Some of them, I soon noticed, were resigned, often bitterly, to being cheated by record companies (not all of them), club owners, and booking agents (there were exceptions).

I remember overhearing an agent on the phone selling Lester Young as if he were a piece of meat. He knew nothing about Pres's music; he was just making another discount sale. One of the most powerful agents, Joe Glaser, had on a wall of his office a large, colored drawing of an antebellum plantation scene. The happy darkies were singing away, some of them plucking banjos. Since Glaser had utterly no sense of humor, I knew this wasn't meant as an ironic symbol of slavery days. After all, though he was patronizingly generous to some of his musicians, Glaser was essentially running his own plantation.

Walking down Broadway one afternoon, I saw Dizzy Gillespie coming toward me. He was smiling broadly. "I just went to see Billy Shaw," Dizzy told me. The Shaw agency booked Gillespie. "You know what I finally told him?" Dizzy said. "I told him, 'Billy, I don't work for you! You work for me!'"

In those years, not many jazz musicians would speak such bold truth to those with the power to decide their economic future. Recordings were vital to get work, and players who had to scramble for a living—waiting for the phone to ring—did not read recording contracts all that carefully. Indeed, if you weren't a lawyer, reading all that legalese would not have revealed what it actually said. I'd ask musicians what their royalty arrangements were, and many of them would laugh mirthlessly, saying, "I get as much of an advance as I can because I know I'll never see any royalties."

Back then, trumpeter Donald Byrd began to educate himself and other musicians on contract law. And some had lawyers read the contract before they signed it. When I was in charge of A&R for Candid Records in the early 1960s, Max Roach came in with Bruce Wright, a formidable attorney who later became a judge. I was glad to see Wright because I didn't want to screw anybody, even inadvertently.

Even now, there are musicians coming up—and even some veterans—who need legal advice. A valuable source is The Jazz Foundation of America (JFA) in New York. I've written about the free medical service—including expensive surgery the foundation provides at Englewood Hospital in New Jersey. But a jazz player can also contact The Jazz Foundation and get free counseling from a lawyer specializing in musicians' rights—including the right to an honest contract. Another pro bono expert available through The Jazz Foundation works for a music publishing company. Such a specialist can illuminate publishing rights and also advise musicians on action to take when a royalty statement doesn't look right.

For many years, the labels on jazz recordings would indicate that some well-known jazz composers had co-writers with whom they had to split the proceeds. These "creative" partners were often managers, agents or record company executives who cut themselves in for a piece of the action in return for getting the artist on the label. For instance, too many of Duke Ellington's works are listed as being co-written by Irving Mills. In those years, Mills, an aggressive music publisher, booked the Ellington band and orchestrated its publicity. In his spare time, he allegedly co-composed such standards as "Mood Indigo."

Musicians who know about The Jazz Foundation can not only connect with these services, but also at the foundation's Monday night jam sessions at the New York musicians union (322 W. 48th Street), younger players are able to network with experienced jazz musicians—experienced in all dimensions of the jazz scene. An indication of the need for this information is that the most instructive sessions at last year's *JazzTimes* Convention were about the business of jazz.

The foundation also has a referral service for callers who want to employ jazz musicians. It's at 322 W. 48th Street, New York, NY 10036. (212-245-3999 or 1-800-532-5267), and it reaches as far as the sounds of the music.

TESTOSTERONE IS NOT
A MUSICAL INSTRUMENT

I n a guest editorial in the March issue of *JazzTimes*, Lara Pellegrinelli wrote that Wynton Marsalis' Lincoln Center Jazz Orchestra has yet to have a full-time female musician. Earlier, Pellegrinelli had composed a scorching, longer indictment in the November 14 *Village Voice*, and that led to a protest rally outside the Lincoln Center benefit gala, organized by singer Joan Bender. The message was: testosterone is not an instrument.

Last summer, I was part of a panel discussion on jazz with, among others, Stanley Crouch and Rob Gibson, then the executive producer and director of Jazz at Lincoln Center. I mentioned that except for singers and pianists, the abiding prejudice against women in jazz still continues–with the Lincoln Center Jazz Orchestra a prime exhibit. My friend, Stanley Crouch, in a characteristic roar, declared, "If you can show me a woman player who can make it, I'll listen to her!" In the front row was a black musician who looked at Stanley, and said, "Last night, at our rehearsal, there was a woman on tenor who played her ass off."

For once, Stanley was silent. But Rob Gibson said that, as Wynton Marsalis ritually points out when asked about the absence of women in his orchestra, players are selected on their merits. Then Gibson added, as a sort of self-absolution, that of the high school jazz musicians who enter Lincoln Center's competition each year, forty percent are young women. That reminded me of Duke Ellington telling me that before the civil rights movement gathered momentum, there were a lot of blacks with college degrees in post-office jobs or working as Pullman porters. That was as far as they could go.

I would recommend several books to Mr. Marsalis and the rest of the officials at the continually expanding jazz operation at Lincoln Center: Sherrie Tucker's *Swing Shift: "All-Girl" Bands of the 1940s* (Duke University Press) and D. Antoinette Handy's *The International Sweethearts of Rhythm* (Scarecrow Press). To see as well as hear that powerfully swinging band, there is a video: *Sweethearts of Rhythm* (Cinema Guild: 212-685-6242). This fall, the University of Illinois Press will publish an updated edition of Marian McPartland's remarkable memoir, which includes profiles of Mary Lou Williams, Paul Desmond, Benny Goodman, and Bill Evans among others. In *All in Good Time* she also writes "The Untold Story of the International Sweethearts of Rhythm." And why aren't their recordings being reissued?

As more and more high schools and colleges and courses in jazz history, those books should be part of the curriculum because, as Marian noted: "Each of us is an individual—unique, different. The kind of life we have lived comes out in our music." That's precisely what Charlie Parker used to say. But the late George Simon insisted, "Women can't play jazz." They don't have the chops. They can't swing. I'd like to give Wynton Marsalis a blindfold test and play not only recordings by the International Sweethearts of Rhythm with tenor saxophonist Vi Burnside, but also parts of *On the Brink* (Arbors Records) by Sherrie Maricle's small combo, Five Play. Also, he ought to hear Israeli tenor saxophonist Anat Cohen, now with Maricle.

At the rally Joan Bender organized outside Lincoln Center, the small band of civil rights demonstrators passed out fliers that contrasted the female version of Jim Crow in the Lincoln Center Jazz Orchestra with liberated orchestras in New York: "Women are in the Metropolitan, Philharmonic, and City Ballet Orchestras because they have: 1) job advertising; 2) blind auditions, in which unknown candidates perform behind a screen; 3) auditions observed by a committee [not just one man, Marsalis, as at Lincoln Center]; and 4) tenure process."

The flier quoted from Pellegrinelli's *Village Voice* article: "Since the adoption of blind auditions, the number of women has risen dramatically in hundreds of orchestras . . . but virtually none of the top mainstream bands—the Smithsonian Jazz Masterworks Orchestra, the ghost bands of Count Basie or Duke Ellington . . . currently employ any female players as permanent members." The manifesto also quotes Billy Taylor, a supporter of this movement for equal time to be heard: "Time won't do it. There has to be an effort."

The effort is underway, and I don't think it's going to be stopped, any more than the black civil rights momentum ahs been slowed. For years, as a reporter on employment discrimination stories, I heard employers say earnestly: "We'd hire blacks, but we can't find qualified applicants." In memory, I heard those voices again when the pickets at Lincoln Center railed against "the myth that there aren't any female jazz musicians competent enough to be in the Lincoln Center Jazz Orchestra. The fact that it never holds auditions, relying on the old boy network of word of mouth recommendations" explains why that myth is still nurtured there.

Years ago, there used to be grudging compliments to odd women jazz musicians: "You play like a man!" One retort might have been: "That's mighty white of you!"

THE RAINBOW
OF COUNTRY MUSIC

BLUES BROTHERS UNDER THE SKIN

In the early 1950s, as I've often noted, I was listening to a pop music station on the radio. Suddenly I was astonished to hear the deep Mississippi blues of Arthur "Big Boy" Crudup. But I was wrong. The announcer came on to say that the singer was someone I'd never heard of—Elvis Presley. Later I learned that Crudup was Presley's favorite blues singer and that Elvis was country before he was rock 'n' roll.

Accordingly, I was no longer surprised at the strong ties between white country music and black blues when Bill Malone, a widely respected historian of country music, noted that Bob Willis—a pioneer of Western swing—"rode nearly fifty miles on horseback to see Bessie Smith in person." He was still in his teens. And one of his first recordings was her "Gulf Coast Blues."

Until the recent release of *From Where I Stand: The Black Experience in Country Music* (three CDs with illuminating notes and photographs), however, I had not fully realized the extensive historical interplay between black and white sources in the creation of country music.

The set, on the Warner Brothers label, was produced by the Country Music Foundation. Of the many stories that are an integral part of the collection, there is a remembrance by Bobby Hebb, a black songwriter and singer. For five years he was a sideman with Roy Acuff, an icon of white country music. Mr. Hebb got to play at country music's fabled Grand Ole Opry.

"That was a school!" says Mr. Hebb. "And there was Hank Williams Sr." (The most personal singer and composer in all of country music.) Mr. Hebb, already immersed in jazz and blues, was instructed by Williams that night in how to write country soul music: "Son, when you write a song, sit down and write it as if you were writin' a letter. Just tell the truth, just like it is. If it hurts you, tell it just how it hurts." Mr. Hebb remembers Williams putting his arm around him, his guitar on his left side, his right arm around the young black performer.

The first disk of *The Black Experience in Country Music* goes back to the years before World War II and focuses on both black and white string bands—the Georgia Yellow Hammers, the Dallas Stringband, the Memphis Sheiks, and the Mississippi Mud Stompers. Among the songs is "Yodeling Fiddling Blues," reflecting the influence of Jimmie Rodgers, the white blues singer and yodeler.

An even more diversified multiculturalism is revealed on this disk, as the notes indicate, in "the relationship between the Georgia Yellow Hammers, an old-time white stringband from Calhoun County in rural North Georgia, and Afro-Cherokee musicians Andrew and Jim Baxter."

The basic aim of *The Black Experience in Country Music* is to break down the false segregation that pervades

American music. Several white jazz musicians were amazed, one night, to find out that Charlie Parker was an admirer of country songs. "Listen to the stories!" he explained. "Listen to the stories!" That anecdote, which originally appeared in one of these reviews, begins the notes for this ecumenical set.

The second CD reveals how personally black singers and instrumentalists have been interpreting white country music. Ray Charles singing Hank Snow's "I'm Movin' On"; Bobby Hebb bringing a new dimension to "Night Train to Memphis," previously popularized by Roy Acuff; and a deeply compelling "Detroit City" sung by Arthur Alexander, eclipsing the original recording by Bobby Bare.

Another lasting fusion of white and black roots is Etta James's "Almost Persuaded." She says she wanted "to show that gospel, country, blues, rhythm and blues, jazz, and rock & roll are all really just one thing." She comes close to showing all that in this recording.

The last CD of the triptych, *Forward with Pride,* begins with Charley Pride, country music's only black superstar. A former baseball player in various Negro Leagues, Pride, the singer, was discovered by white country performer Red Sovine. After his first hit, 1966's "The Snakes Crawl at Night," a grim tale of the consequences of adultery, Mr. Pride was on the charts for a long time. He still tours but doesn't have to, being involved in banking, music publishing, and other enterprises.

The final disk also includes such weavers of black and white textures and storytelling rhythms as the Pointer Sisters, Cleve Francis (who is also a practicing cardiologist), and Barrence Whitfield, who sings Merle Haggard's song of besieged interracial love, "Irma Jackson."

In the notes, Bill Ivey, director of the Country Music Foundation, accurately says: "What is most striking about this collection of recordings is the ease with which authentic country performers emerge from the hands and voices of African-American interpreters, and the ease with which country compositions fit the demands of rhythm & blues." A black annotator, Ron Wynn, adds: "Since music was far from a priority or interest of my parents, I had no one to tell me that being black meant you couldn't find drama, passion and beauty in the songs of George Jones or Merle Haggard."

"From Where I Stand: The Black Experience in Country Music" is available in retail record stores or by mail order from the Country Music Foundation.

WILLIE NELSON:
HONKY TONK GYPSY

As usual, Willie Nelson was on the road again, calling me from his band bus. At sixty-seven, he plays from 200 to 250 dates a year because—as he sings in his recording "On the Road Again"—he "can't wait to keep going to places I've never been, seeing things I may never see again."

On the phone he was eager to talk about a project he'd long wanted to do, and has finally accomplished—an entirely instrumental CD built around his guitar playing. His impressive, cumulative record sales are based largely on his singing and compositions, and most of his lay admirers take his picking for granted. But country musicians know better.

So you'd think the pre-eminent star of a hugely popular genre could get a record company to do whatever he wanted. But in order to get a no-vocals disk off the ground, Mr. Nelson had to form his own label, Pedernales Records, which, in partnership with Freefalls Entertainment, recently brought out *Night and Day*.

Jazz Influences

There has often been a supple sense of jazz phrasing and rhythm in some of Mr. Nelson's previous recordings, but this venture lets him improvise more freely and makes clear his devotion to the passionate Gypsy jazz guitarist Django Reinhardt, the only non-American to establish himself in the pantheon of jazzmen.

Reinhardt lost two fingers from his left hand early on in his career during a caravan fire, but, Mr. Nelson told me, "he could still do the most incredible things. Django was the greatest guitarist ever—what he could do with melody, his tone, his style." As for the very distinctive sound of Willie's guitar, Ray Benson, leader of Asleep at the Wheel, gets it right: "a cross between Django's gypsy jazz and a Mexican guitar."

In Abbott, Texas, the town of 200 people where he grew up, Willie Nelson heard not only classic country music, as on the Grand Ole Opry radio broadcasts, but also the "Western swing" of Bob Willis. And later, when he worked the honky tonks, jazz-laced country sounds and rhythms were commonplace. To this twangy subculture of musicians, the French-speaking Reinhardt was no stranger. Merle Haggard, another country-music icon, told me years ago, "My big jazz love was Django Reinhardt. I loved everything he did."

On *Night and Day* there are two performances directly connected with Reinhardt, "Vous et Moi" and "Nuages." On the latter, Mr. Nelson pays a deeply affectionate if wordless, lyrical tribute to the nonpareil Django. But despite its fixation on this hero from another country, the disk is filled out by pop standards—the title track, as well as "All the Things You Are," "September in the Rain," "Honeysuckle Rose."

I had not realized that such standards were standard fodder in the often tumultuous clubs were Mr. Nelson served his apprenticeship. "When I was playing every night in Texas," he explained, "you had to play a lot of these tunes. The folks wanted to hear them—sometimes twice a night."

Rough and Ready

Mr. Nelson manifestly enjoys himself on every track here. He stretches out on the guitar and trades off with veteran members of his traveling troupe—including drummer Paul English and his own older sister, Bobbie, whose piano playing evokes the rough and ready ambience of the clubs where she and her brother first confirmed their true vocations. (Mr. Nelson plans a future Pedernales disk featuring his indispensable sibling on honky-tonk and boogie-woogie numbers.)

Alongside Willie, a special, swing pleasure in *Night and Day* is Johnny Gimble, a master of country-music jamming on fiddle and mandolin. Mr. Gimble comes from the same part of Texas as Mr. Nelson, and they worked together, says Willie, "many nights when we were coming up. And as Django is to me, Stephane Grappelli is to Johnny." Grappelli was the jazz violinist whose recordings with Reinhardt have never lost their exuberant immediacy.

Soon after my conversation with Willie Nelson from his bus, he stopped briefly at Westport, Connecticut, for an evening open-air concert. There was a huge crowd, as for all his dates. The concert lasted for more than two hours—short for him—and for a half hour afterward, while the sound equipment and drums were being packed into the bus. Willie signed autographs and joked with his fans.

I had never seen him live before, although I have most of his recordings. But just as no recording fully equaled the impact of Louis Armstrong or Count Basie's band in a live performance, I was struck by the sheer power that Mr. Nelson and his band project in person. The often subtle dynamics of his voice and guitar on recordings gives way to a forceful, swinging presence as his country, blues, gospel, and jazz roots merge so that intimate songs such as "Funny How Time Slips Away" and "Night Life" become proclamations rather than interior monologues.

Bobbie Nelson's two-handed piano keeping the beat rolling and rocking like a train's, made me imagine what a night in Dodge saloon must have been like. But suddenly, it was as if time stopped: The volume lowered and Willie Nelson distilled loneliness for us: "Come lay down by my side, all I'm taking is your time. I don't care if it's right or wrong, let the devil take tomorrow. Tonight I need a friend." Later, after "Whiskey River" and "On the Road Again" brought the audience out of its reveries, Mr. Nelson once more softened the night with Django's "Nuages."

Another new Pedernales/Freefalls release recalls the rowdier nights of Willie's youth in the honky tonks. In *Honky Tonk Heroes* Mr. Nelson and his longtime comrades Kris Kristofferson, Waylon Jennings, and Billy Joe Shaver sing of long-ago rowdy nights, tender women, and the spirit of honky-tonk hero Hank Williams, "who sang every song lookin' straight at me." So does Willie.

THOSE CHEATIN' HEARTS

Country singers excel in songs about "slipping around" or "crossing the line." It's a honky-tonk world of adultery in its ingeniously secluded forms, with a constant obbligato of guilty pleasure—from overly requited love ("She won't leave me alone till it's too late to go home") to ultimately defiant confessions ("Hell, yes, I cheated, even though it was wrong, but she gave me somethin' I've been missing at home").

In *The Wandering Eyes: Songs of Forbidden Love,* a lively company of Texas singers trade stories about carnal sin on the sly. The recording was produced by Dave Sanger, the drummer with Asleep at the Wheel, a group that fuses swinging warmth and wit. (The label is Lazy S.O.B. Recordings in Austin, Texas, 512-480-0765.)

Says Mr. Sanger: "this is not a compilation or a tribute album, unless you call it a tribute to indiscretion." The idea originated between takes at a recording session, when Mr. Sanger, who has been in country music for only twelve years, heard a colleague, Jason Roberts, singing some vintage songs Mr. Sanger had never heard, "I thought," Mr. Sanger says, "that if I don't know these pure cheating songs, I'm sure bunches of people haven't heard them either."

Not only country aficionados are likely to be drawn to these scenes of the illicit life force. The songs are so open and honest that they speak to anybody of any background—from the lowliest streets to the highest office in the land—about uncontrollable desire.

Among the singers is Dale Watson; long one of the most powerfully understated country bards, he ought to be far more recognized than he is. Also convincingly assuming the identities of the various dissemblers are Kelly Willis, Rosie Flores, Chris O'Connell, Ted Roddy, and Jason Roberts (whose obscure songs of crossing the line first stirred Mr. Sanger to assemble these shadow plays of forbidden love).

The accompaniment is in the easeful, attentive groove of the best of country music's rhythm sections. Along with members of Asleep at the Wheel, there are alumni of the Waylon Jennings, George Strait, and Dale Watson bands. Their rhythms are for dancers as well as listeners—gently but irresistibly moving the partners into foreordained intimacy.

The lyrics, like these form "In Some Room Above the Street," tenderly sung by Ms. Flores, show the settings:

"There's no place for us to hide in the neon world outside
So I suppose we'll always be
In some room above the street . . .
It's strange that love can be so sweet
In some room above the street."

And there is concern—part guilt, part natural empathy—for the deceived other woman, the one with a wedding ring:

> *"But if she wants your love tonight*
> *Don't turn away, don't hurt her pride*
> *Just close your eyes and think of me*
> *In some room above the street."*

Jimmy Rushing, a longtime singer with Count Basie, once told me that all lasting songs, in all genres, were "he-she" songs. Maybe not all, but most—from Cole Porter to Merle Haggard. Still, no form of music focuses more often and intensely on hidden passion than country music. As in this guilty admission:

> *"Like thieves and beggars when we meet*
> *Awake before the break of day*
> *And like the night we steal away."*

And great, continual care must be taken not to give the game away, to wipe away the "Cheatin' Traces":

> *"I must check my hand, make sure my wedding band's*
> *   still on*
> *I must wash my face, make sure that all the lipstick's*
> *   gone*
> *I must sweep the car, make sure no hair pin's left behind*
> *Before I get home I must lose all those cheating traces."*

One extraordinary night, in a crowded club, I listened to Mr. Haggard singing many kinds of "he-she" songs that sounded so personal they could be part of his autobiography. Later, talking to him, I found that some of those songs were indeed mined from his life.

Not all country songs are that confessional, however. Randy Travis once told me that some of his songs came from listening to people talk in bars, and those conversations, out of those real lives, became part of the "he-she" stories he tells.

On this CD, the authenticity of the language and the rhythms marks the difference between classic country music and the mechanical "crossover" songs that make the charts and whose words and music are largely fungible. The stories here sound as if they were overheard, and maybe were:

> *"For a long time now we've lived together*
> *But still we've been alone*
> *We lived inside a house, but it's never been a home*
> *And all I took from her was love that we no longer share*
> *It didn't seem so bad 'cause I didn't know you cared."*

When I was traveling with the Flatt and Scruggs band through the South, back in the days when classic country music was the only kind, I told one of the players how impressed I was at the rapt attention of the audiences at every stop.

"Sure," he said. "We know who they are, and they know that. They come to hear us tell them about their lives."

DELBERT MCCLINTON:
LONE STAR TROUBADOUR

Years ago at the Lone Star, a country-music night-club in New York, I heard an itinerant Texan, Delbert McClinton, sing the blues, rhythm and blues, rock, and honky-tonk country songs for nearly two hours without stopping. He had the energy of Kansas City's Big Joe Turner and the air of a midnight rambler. I've been following his fragmented career ever since. For a while I lost sight of him, but now he's come roaring back, showing up in May on five separate Billboard album charts—blues, country, independent albums, the top 20, and Internet sales.

Born in Lubbock, Texas, in 1940, he grew up in Fort Worth, and as a youngster became immersed in the whirl of Western swing, blues, jazz, rock, and country sounds that abounded in dance halls and honky-tonks there. By the late 1950s, he was working in honky-tonks on the Jacksboro Highway, a scene he described to me recently. "There was a screen up between the band and the audience. Sometimes bottles were flying in the air. The customers came out to roar after the stresses of the day. That music was white people's blues."

On-the-Job Training

In his early twenties, he says, "I got lucky." His band was booked by a black promoter to play for Blue Monday nights at the Skyline Ballroom in Fort Worth. "Mine was the only white band there. It was the greatest education I could possibly have had, playing behind my heroes"— blues performers Jimmy Reed, Sonny Boy Williams, B.B. King, Joe Turner, Lightnin' Hopkins, Bobby Bland. Though Mr. McClinton can be a compelling guitarist, his strength as an instrumentalist is on the blues harmonica, "the harp." "I got on-the-job training," he told me, "from Sonny Boy Williams and Jimmy Reed at the Skyline."

He left Texas for a while as a sideman in a rock band that played England, where John Lennon heard him and took a few harmonica lessons. Though he returned to the Lone Star State, he's been on the road ever since, first with other groups and eventually on his own, driven by what Merle Haggard calls "white line fever."

Some of his twenty-seven albums have done well, but as John Burnett noted in an interview with Mr. McClinton in July on National Public Radio, "he had a remarkable run of bad luck with record companies. . . . The parent company dumps the smaller label to which he signed, or the label declares bankruptcy." The period I lost track of him was when, for five years, he refused to record for a company that wouldn't release him from a bad contract.

But Delbert McClinton has had other problems of his own making. "I was livin' a life," he told Mr. Burnett, "where all I was after was the next little bit of cocaine, a different woman every night. I was trying to escape from my life. To put some of those things to rest, I've had to write songs about them."

Now Mr. McClinton is in control not only of his life, but of his music, taking charge of his new album, *Nothing Personal* (New West Records; www.newwestrecords.com), from beginning to end. Writing or co-writing all the songs, he took ten and a half months, "living with the songs. I can't say that about any other record I've ever done. I made it for me, and not for any particular radio format. Music is getting so homogenized it's driving me crazy."

It was *Nothing Personal* that gave added meaning to the term "crossover" hit, spreading across five Billboard charts. It's not only Mr. McClinton's best recording, it's a country-music classic at a time when that genre has come close to sounding like elevator music. The notes contain the complete lyrics, and some of them rank with the most durable of Merle Haggard's, which is like saying that an alto saxophonist has cut a recording that can stand alongside those of Johnny Hodges, or of Charlie Parker playing the blues.

Personal Stories

This record is also Mr. McClinton's most personal, despite the ironic title. There is the ultimate broken love affair, "When Rita Leaves." Having been "done wrong," she drove his sky-blue ragtag Mustang into the night and, dousing it with kerosene, "burned that pony to the ground on the desert in New Mexico." Her mother tells the stricken narrator, "You're lucky all she broke was your heart. You better just let her go."

"It sounds," I said to Mr. McClinton, "like you've had your Rita." He paused. "Well," he said, "pretty close."

His songs, he went on, "don't always come out of my life, but from what I've heard and seen. All you got to do is look around and hear the stories." He tells one in "Desperation": "she's sleepin' in the kitchen on the hardwood floor / Said it fixed her back, it don't hurt no more / She's lookin' real good / But she's havin' some trouble with her knees."

Describing how he writes a song, Mr. McClinton said, "I like to have three or four different things you can isolate as you listen. Like in 'Desperation': There's the vocal, what the drums are doing, what the guitar is saying, and the riff. A blues or jazz riff on the guitar gets me motivated. And I try to write lyrics as simple as I can, but in a way no one else is writing."

He may be analytical, but his legions of enthusiastic fans react viscerally to his performances. As Mr. Burnett reported: "There's a local Austin custom where certain female fans throw their undergarments onto the stage." And there's an annual Delbert McClinton Caribbean cruise, for which some 750 admirers pay $1,400 to hear him along with other performers such as, in the past, Asleep at the Wheel.

In *Nothing Personal*, Delbert McClinton sums it all up: "Got all my snakes back into the box / Now I'm where I wanna be / Sittin' here watchin' the rain."

DALE WATSON:

HARD COUNTRY, SOFT HEART

n 1994, country-music singer and composer Dale Watson, whose uncertain career in California and Texas I had been following over the years, decided to retire his guitar and enroll in a Texas community college to learn enough about repairing motorcycles to land a day job. Both the road and the roadhouse were in his blood: As a kid, he'd accompanied his father, a truck driver who doubled as a singer in truck stops and cafés in rural west Tennessee. And his uncle Jim had played guitar with the legendary country star Merle Travis.

Mr. Watson began writing songs at twelve, made his first recording two years later and was soon playing at clubs. But by the early 1990s he had become discouraged by the increasing blandness of what passes for country music on the radio, in record stores and, much of the time, in Nashville and decided to call it quits.

It didn't last long. When a European record company asked him to make an album, he returned to his first calling. Among the sets he later recorded was the 1998 *Truckin' Sessions*—the result of a two-year tour playing truck stops. As usual, Mr. Watson didn't get too much play on mainstream country radio stations, which regarded him as "too country." Those stations seldom even play the nonpareil Merle Haggard, who has influenced Mr. Watson.

Big in Europe

There are still listeners, however, who yearn for undiluted honky-tonk stories that reflect their own regrets and hopes, and that audience accounts for Mr. Watson's 250 or so appearances a year—including tours of Europe, where he has many admirers who have never directly savored the ambience of an actual honky-tonk.

Last year, Dale Watson released what is called in the business "a career record"—*Every Song I Write Is for You* (Audium, www.dalewatson.com, and in record stores). In Music Row: Nashville's Industry Publication, John Hood writes, "I'll be listening to this album in twenty years." I expect it will have a longer life span than that.

But every song was written for the late Terri Herbert, a lawyer on the staff of Texas' attorney general, whom musicians in Austin had counted on for help with their legal problems. She and Mr. Watson met at a party, immediately fell in love and made plans to get married. But on September 15, 2000, while driving to Houston to meet Mr. Watson, she fell asleep at the wheel.

Devastated, "trying to cope without going insane," Mr. Watson began to write songs for and about a woman who, in just four months, had "turned my world around. The songs just flooded in," he says. "I wasn't even thinking about putting them out. These are the best songs I've written, but I recorded them for me."

He first went into the studio a month after Herbert's death, and recorded ten of the fourteen songs on the CD. But he fell into a precipitous depression, and on December 28 that year, in an Austin motel room, he washed down a quart of vodka and a quantity of sleeping pills. "I kinda went crazy. I tried to kill myself and ended up in the nuthouse." (He committed himself to a state hospital.)

Memories of a Lost Love

After treatment, as he began "to appreciate what we had together instead of just mourning," Mr. Watson hit the road again, including a tour of Europe. Meanwhile, he and Terri Herbert's mother started a Terri Herbert Foundation that awards college scholarships to high-school students in single-parent homes. Mr. Watson's proceeds from *Every Song I Write Is for You* go to the foundation, which also helps find shelters for abused women and children, a concern of Herbert's.

The memories of the incandescent four months with her make up, Mr. Watson says, "a love-song album with no apologies." In the unusually wide-ranging music magazine *No Depression*, Barry Mazor accurately makes the point that "this is not a dark, introspective confessional, but an often sweet, sometimes even breezy collection of unmitigated love songs."

Backed by the kind of Western-swing band that travels with Merle Haggard, Mr. Watson's lyrical, conversational baritone evokes the spirit of Terri Herbert in the album's opening song: "You like to sway to the music / You like the feel of a tune." And that also describes the natural, inviting rhythms of his singing.

On his other recordings, Mr. Watson brings the listener into the rambunctiousness of the honky-tonks. But here, although there are some joyful reminiscences of those four months, the mood is often subdued, the way things get in a club when most the revelers have gone. In "I See the Future," Mr. Watson and a stranger trade photographs of women they've lost. "We talked about our struggle to go on."

In another song, "I'd Deal with the Devil to Get Her Back," Mr. Watson sings:

> *"I talk to the man above but he ain't listenin' up*
> *So I'd deal with the Devil to get her back.*
> *He can throw my soul into a fiery hole*
> *To burn for all eternity*
> *Just for one more night to have her by my side*
> *And hold on to her, not just her memory."*

When he first released this album, Mr. Watson wondered what kind of radio play these unadorned, spontaneously personal country songs would get. "We'll see," he said, "if radio's too scared to provoke any real emotion, because there's nothing more real than this."

Nick Hunter, president of Audium Records, which has done extensive promotion of the recording, told *Billboard* back in June: "In the beginning, mainstream radio will probably look at us and laugh. They'll probably think it's too country, which is fine with me."

And indeed, mainstream "soft" country radio has not been too interested. But radio play has been very good in Texas and around the country on the more than ninety-five stations in the Americana format (traditional country and other roots music). Undaunted, Mr. Hunter says: "The good thing about Dale is you know what you're getting. There aren't going to be any Celtic waltzes on this record."

As for thirty-eight-year-old Dale Watson: "As long as I'm able to do what I'm doing, that's all I care about."

FROM 1970S LONGHAIR ROCKERS TO
BLUEGRASS ICONS

For years, jazz friends have questioned my deep affection for authentic country music—not the denatured elevator music that has been coming out of Nashville for the past forty years. Charlie Parker, also a devotee, used to explain to his puzzled colleagues, "Listen to the stories!" And, citing Count Basie's basic definition of jazz as "foot-tapping music," I have recommended recordings by Earl Scruggs, who reinvented the banjo as Charlie Parker had the alto saxophone.

Now, a classic country-music cross-generational jam session has been reissued and remastered after thirty years—with several new tracks and in-studio dialogue—and its 36,000 in sales since March indicate that there is a discerning audience for celebrations of traditional music-making.

Will the Circle Be Unbroken (a two-CD Capitol Records set) had an improbable beginning. A country-rock group, the Nitty Gritty Dirt Band, more attuned to roots music than most such bands of its generation, was playing its first Nashville gig in 1970. In the audience was Earl Scruggs, his wife, Louise, and their sons. A year later, "this bunch of longhaired West Coast boys"—as country music patriarch Roy Acuff was to call them—mustered the courage to ask Scruggs if he'd record a song with the Dirt Band.

I came to know Scruggs when, years ago, I traveled on the bus with the band he co-led with Lester Flatt, through Alabama and Tennessee. Generous of spirit and disdainful of categories in music, he surprised some of his country fans back then by appearing in concert with anti-Vietnam War protester Joan Baez. Characteristically, he agreed to record with the California longhairs and allowed them to use his name to persuade other musicians and singers of his generation to join him in the studio.

Along with Roy Acuff, Mother Maybelle Carter (of the legendary Carter Family), Doc Watson, Merle Travis, Jimmy Martin, the passionate fiddler Vassar Clements, and other veterans of the Grand Ole Opry came along. Refusing, however, was Bill Monroe, the Charlie Parker of bluegrass, who disdained practitioners of rock.

While this was a Nitty Gritty Dirt Band recording, the band deferred to its guests, playing secondary roles in the six-day session. As Randy Lewis noted in the Los Angeles Times review of this reissue of *Will the Circle Be Unbroken*: "One Nashville publication of the time labeled the 'Circle' participants dinosaurs because their music seemed light-years removed from the smooth music . . . coming out of Music City."

But to the young admirers of the "dinosaurs," delighted to be accompanying them, the experience was—as singer-guitarist Jeff Hanna of the Dirt Band said—"as if we were being welcomed into a family. It started," he told Randy Lewis, "with Earl Scruggs and his family, but it extended to that entire family of musicians we met on those sessions."

Indeed, Jimmy Martin, the penetrating singer and leader of the Sunny Mountain Boys, wanted to hire those "hippies." The mixture of ages and styles resembled that of Norman Granz's Jazz at the Philharmonic (JATP) concerts; but while the JATP sessions were intensely competitive—"cutting sessions" in the parlance of the time—the singers and players in this extended country family were at ease in each other's company, as can also be heard in the conversations between takes.

At one point, listening to Roy Acuff declare his philosophy of recording before moving into his song "The Precious Jewel," I remembered Duke Ellington telling me that he tried not to do more than two or three takes on a recording because he'd rather have the music fresh, even with a few mistakes.

Thus Acuff instructed his new colleagues: "I'll tell you a little secret of my policy in the studio. Put everything you have into it. Don't say 'we'll play it over and do it again,' because every time you go through it, you lose just a little something."

It was not only Roy Acuff who held nothing back. The others also let go, unencumbered by smothering banks of violins behind them as in "countrypolitan" sessions. And the songs and breakdowns were not carefully chosen to make the playlists of the stolidly "mainstream" country-music stations, along with the Billboard charts. These were for the ages:

A. P. Carter's "Keep on the Sunnyside" and "I'm Thinking Tonight of My Blue Eyes"; Hank Williams's "Honky Tonkin'"; Scruggs's "Foggy Mountain Breakdown"; Travis's "Nine Pound Hammer"; and Martin's "Losin' You (Might Be the Best Thing Yet)."

And—just as Jazz at the Philharmonic had everyone on for the climax—the entire cast joined in on "Will the Circle Be Unbroken," the Carter Family's anthem of eternal faith. (In October, Capitol will release Volume 3 of *Will the Circle Be Unbroken*. Volume 2, with a similar multi-generational cast, was released in 1989 on Universal/MCA, but has not been reissued. The new Vol. 3, recorded this May and June, includes Johnny Cash, Ricky Skaggs, Willie Nelson, Alison Krauss, and Earl Scruggs.)

It took the original set twenty-six years to sell a million copies as it reached into generations of listeners and players. In the May-June issue of the roots music magazine *No Depression* musician Jon Weisberger wrote that when he was seventeen, he found "this touchstone and textbook" in his small-town record shop, and that experience was multiplied by many more players for whom the circle remains unbroken.

With the soundtrack of "O Brother, Where Art Thou?" having astonished the record industry and country-music radio stations by selling some five million copies, Capitol Records' marketing vice president, Fletcher Foster, told Billboard of his hopes for the regenerated *Circle*: "It is a kind of circle, coming back around at a time when bluegrass music and roots music are back in the forefront."

Don Rigsby:
The Sound of His
Kentucky Heritage

I n a time when it is a blessing not to be able to make out much of the lyrics of the music on the radio, and most so-called country-music stations find Hank Williams or Merle Haggard too close to the bone, it is a deep pleasure to hear the clear-as-country-water voice and soulful mandolin of Don Rigsby. He came from Isonville, Kentucky, hard to find in gazetteers, to be a compelling force in the lively bluegrass tradition.

When he's not performing in a club or concert, Mr. Rigsby is the director of the Kentucky Center for Traditional Music at Morehead State University, Morehead, Kentucky. He tells me that his slogan as an academic practicing what he teaches is: "educating, preserving, entertaining."

That department, describing "What our traditional music is and is not," clearly defines Mr. Rigsby's Sugar Hill Records CDs (*Midnight Call, A Vision* and *Empty Old Mailbox*, available at sugarhillrecords.com, Amazon.com, and many record stores): "our working definition of traditional music embraces bluegrass, historical folk, old timey, mountain, gospel, and other music forms spanning the full range of acoustic instrumentation and vocal presentation. . . . The mandolin is featured in our logo because our brand of traditional music does not include the slick, pop-oriented 'Nashville sound' of today's mainstream country music."

Don Rigsby, born in 1968, was already listening on records to the haunting echoes of old English ballads in the singing of Ralph Stanley. Then, on his sixth birthday, the boy was taken to nearby Ashland to see Mr. Stanley sing "Little Maggie," which the child had learned to sing from a Stanley record the year before. The boy actually met Ralph Stanley backstage. Now, on the last track of Don Rigsby's *A Vision,* there is the lead vocalist, the legendary Mr. Stanley, in the riveting gospel song "Vision of a Golden Crown."

On that album, "Higher Than I," an a cappella solo by Mr. Rigsby is one of the most emotionally penetrating musical experiences I've had. My only religion is the U.S. Constitution, but Mr. Rigsby made me understand what Kierkegaard called "the leap into faith" that powers much of the traditional music of Kentucky and Appalachia.

Writing of Mr. Rigsby's extraordinarily resilient tenor voice in the notes to "A Vision," Ron Thomason describes it exactly: "No tricks, pitch-perfect, unworldly attention to detail, and yet quickness and finesse where you don't dare to expect it. . . . His is more than a voice with the 'bark left on.' His roots show above the ground. His voice is the fiber from which a new forest will spring."

Teaching at Morehead, of which Mr. Rigsby is an alumnus, lets him keep "a foot in the past and a foot in the future," he says. (When he was a student there, mountain music was looked down on by the academics.) In addition to his current course in vocal harmony—of which his recordings present a master class—next semester he will teach "music listening classes." If public television and C-Span cared about distinctive culture, they would have cameras at Morehead's satellite college in West Liberty filming that class.

Mr. Rigsby is also enthusiastically involved at Morehead in "The Sound of Our Heritage" concert series that, in the fall, is aimed at middle- and high-school students from eastern Kentucky. Mr. Rigsby, however, welcomes anyone of any age who wants to learn how to sing and play traditional music.

He told me of a woman who came to his vocal harmony class because, although she was very much wanted to sing in her church, she was discouraged from doing so because she didn't know how to join in. "I told her," Mr. Rigsby said, " 'You just come right in, honey, and we'll figure it out.' It turned out she had a beautiful voice but didn't know how to harmonize." Now she does.

Don Rigsby is far from unknown outside of Kentucky. As a sideman, he became an influential force in the bluegrass world playing with the Bluegrass Cardinals, J.D. Crowe and the New South, and the Lonesome River Band. He was twice a Grammy nominee, and twice winner of the Society for the Preservation of Bluegrass Music of America Traditional Male Vocalist of the Year award. And his *A*

Vision CD won the Association for Independent Music's award for best Southern and Bluegrass Gospel album.

On "Dust to Dust," on his *Empty Old Mailbox* CD, Mr. Rigsby's lead vocal, the harmony singing, and the acoustic instrumental accompaniment is of a sheer, enveloping beauty. Mr. Rigsby practices his faith not only in such songs but also in attendance at his church, the Primitive Baptist Church.

Throughout his recordings, the acoustic accompaniment on fiddle, guitar, Dobro, banjo, bass, and his own mandolin is so finely attuned to the signing in spirit, mood and dynamics that I sometimes play the music again to focus on the seamlessness of this ageless way of telling stories.

Mr. Rigsby tells of daily life and loss. In *The Midnight Call* CD, there is "Dyin' to Hold Her Again":

> *"He drags into work, unaware*
> *of the proof on his breath*
> *Most men would get fired*
> *for puttin' the boss to the test.*
> *But everyone knows his story*
> *and they sympathize*
> *With a man who loves a woman*
> *who left without saying goodbye."*

And, in "What Lays Down the Road":

> *"You say that you still love me*
> *But, I don't feel it when we kiss*
> *We're just going through the motions*
> *And I can't live like this."*

In the songs he chooses by other contemporary traditionalists, and those he himself writes, Mr. Rigsby turns these "ordinary" experiences into the universals of existence, as in the stories of black blues bards, flamenco singers and guitarists, and the leaps into faith by chazans in orthodox synagogues. And, of course, they are in old English ballads in the mists of Mr. Rigsby's memory, as he sings "Blood on My Hands" in a Kentucky version:

> *"Come here, Jane, try to understand*
> *Why I can't die with blood on my hands.*
> *This blood once flowed through*
> *   your brother's veins.*
> *The Lord forgave me, can you*
> *   forgive me, Jane?"*

THE FARTHER RAINBOW

AMERICAN FOLK SONGS, DIRECT FROM THE FIELD

L uther Strong, a fiddler in Hazard, Kentucky, made a field recording, "Glory in the Meetinghouse," for the Library of Congress 60 years ago, and it's still a driving, resounding, foot-tapping delight. For many years after, his daughter recalls, "he'd get up early in the morning and play." Some of the songs were "old, sad tunes. He'd have such a far away look when he'd play them."

Most of the traditional songsters, as they were called, and players are gone. I used to collect their recordings—struck by the force of their presence and the haunting, dreamlike aura of their stories, many of which were rooted in Great Britain centuries ago. But each of these folk enliveners of the past brought his or her own memories and desires to the old tunes, sad or lively.

The most diversely dramatic and illuminating collection of the American folk music heritage is the newly released *A Treasury of Library of Congress Field Recordings* (Rounder Records, 617-354-0700). There are thirty tracks, and the vivid traditionalists are black convicts, white banjo virtuosi, American Indians, black children at play, street singers conjugating the blues, the Alabama

Sacred Harp Singers, and a surprise visitor—known until now only as a distinguished jurist—Judge Learned Hand, singing of the "Iron Merrimac," the iron-clad warship that took on the armored Monitor ship during the Civil War. Stephen Wade, who selected the recordings and wrote the superbly lucid notes, says of Judge Hand that "he sounds very much like the typical Adirondack Mountain balladeer."

A folk song I heard years ago, Vera Hall's rendition of "Another Man Done Gone," has never quite left me. Beyond sadness, it makes palpable a loss that cannot be restored. ("Another man done gone from the country farm, I didn't know his name.")

Hall was recorded in 1940 in Livingston, Alabama, by John Lomax, who, along with his son, Alan, did most of these field recordings, urgently following leads through the South for the vital signs of living traditions. The considerable advantage of having recorded this music where people actually lived—and the sound is quite good—has been noted by Mr. Wade: "These field recordings breathe with on-going life. In the background, kitchen clocks tick, trucks drive by, and roosters crow. Children laugh, and occasionally a performer or his neighbor interrupts a song to talk."

Woody Guthrie is heard in a song from the ballad collection of Francis James Child—ballads that had been sung in Britain before the age of printing. Guthrie, bringing American colors and rhythms to the song, says "hello" to his daughter Sue as she walks by during the recording. And Guthrie speaks of the dynamics of the oral tradition now as well as then: "Sometimes you hear a tune and catch some of the words, and for a long time you go around with it roaring through your head like a lost steamboat."

When I was a kid, Sonny Terry's harmonica would go roaring through my head like a freight train. In this set, Terry was recorded by Alan Lomax in that cross-cultural meeting place New York City. Terry sounds—as Mr. Wade notes—like "a wailing child, barking search dogs, falsetto whoops," while the harmonica engages in "sliding, bending, snapping . . . single-note chokes, wah-wah effects, tongue blocks, chord chugging, open and closed throat constructions, and hand-cupped notes." As Thelonious Monk used to say, there are some things they can't teach you in a conservatory.

And that includes the field holler. Before the blues, a solitary field hand, needing to speak to someone, if only himself, would holler up to the sky. These unaccompanied declarations of weariness or frustration or determination eventually became the foundation for vocal blues. The lonely improvisations turned voices in unexpected directions and transmutations. The black hollers, with their "vocal slides, wavering tones and the leaping of whole registers," call to mind and ear Jewish cantors.

From Parchman prison in Parchman, Mississippi, John Lomax sent "Diamond Joe," a field holler by Charlie Butler, into the world. Lomax believed, as did his son, that in isolated communities—like prisons—there were a lot of compelling unknown artists. The Lomaxes lifted some of them beyond prison walls.

As Alan Lomax emphasized in his books, the music moved around, even if some of the performers didn't, and the traditions became interwoven—black influences on white themes and white stories taking on black forms. For example, the Nashville Washboard Band absorbed an eighteenth-century fiddle tune from England and flavored it with the colors and swing of jazz. And so, "Soldier's Joy" leaps across the centuries in jazz time.

The Library of Congress's involvement in folk music in all its forms began in 1928. Carl Engle, chief of the Library of Congress Music Division, declared: "This centralized collection should comprise all the poems and melodies that have sprung from our soil or have been transplanted here, and have been handed down, often with manifold changes, from generation to generation, as a precious possession of our folk."

Some of us can personalize folk sounds and stories from cultures other than our own. There are klezmer players who, looking for some kind of roots, began as bluegrass banjo pickers, then found their own Jewish past.

For all their talk of multiculturalism and the joys of diversity, many places of higher learning are actually bristling enclaves of single-interest polemics. To get a real introduction to the illuminating surprises of cultural interplay, the students in these courses ought to have access to *A Treasure of Library of Congress Field Recordings.*

FOLK LIVES, THANKS TO
THE SONGCATCHERS

I n 1966, I was talking with Bob Dylan about the surprising resurgence of interest in centuries-old British ballads that had taken root in Appalachia and suddenly made Joan Baez a star—her first album for Vanguard Records in 1960, with such venerable hit songs as "Silver Dagger" and "Mary Hamilton," having earned more than $1 million.

"Traditional music is too unreal to die—songs about roses growing out of people's brains and lovers who are geese and swans who turn into angels," Dylan said.

All during the 1960s and for some years after, I'd hear in clubs and concerts Jean Ritchie, Susan Reed, and other songcatchers—an Appalachian term for those who collect and otherwise keep alive such songs as "Barbara Allen" and "Conversation with Death" ("Oh what is this, I cannot see / An icy hands takes hold on me.")

Both songs are part of *Songcatcher*, on the revived Vanguard Records label, now a division of the Welk Music Group, founded by Lawrence Welk, the easy-listening band leader and television luminary who had few fans in Appalachia. The label now has a lively repertory of jazz, country, blues, and bluegrass, among other forms of what folklorist Alan Lomax called "the rainbow of American music."

Songcatcher is the soundtrack for the film of the same name about a fictional woman music professor who ventures into the Appalachian mountains to research the music there. The character is based on Olive Dame Campbell who, with her minister husband, came to the cabins and hidden valleys ("hollers") in 1908 to find what eventually became the basis for her John C. Campbell Folk School in Brasstown, North Carolina.

Her collection, published by English musicologist Cecil Sharp in 1915—along with the earlier "The English and Scottish Popular Ballads" compiled by Francis James Child—fueled the folk revival, nurturing Baez, Dylan, and scores of coffeehouse singers and academic folklorists.

Maggie Greenwald, the film's writer-director, prepared by going to the Blue Ridge Mountains of North Carolina along with her husband, composer David Mansfield, who became involved in *Songcatcher*. Says Mr. Mansfield: "Music was everywhere—on people's porches, in the back of drugstores. There were old people singing centuries-old ballads and ten-year-old fiddlers learning new songs."

The soundtrack on Vanguard includes such of those centuries-old ballads and their American transformations as "Fair and Tender Ladies," "Wayfaring Stranger," "The Cuckoo Bird," "Mary of the Wild Moor," and "Wind and Rain." Also in the spirit of these enduring tales there are contemporary stories—Dolly Parton's "When Love Is

New," and "Sounds of Loneliness," sung by another distinctive country-music figure, Patty Loveless.

The singers chosen for the soundtrack are seldom heard on today's top forty country music radio stations because they are so attuned to the music still being reborn in Appalachia that they could go down now and sit on the porches and at the back of the drugstores. Among them: Emmylou Harris, Roseanne Cash, Iris Dement, Emmy Rossum, Pat Carroll, Deana Carter, Maria McKee, Sara Evans. And Hazel Dickens, long renowned in folk and country circles, is in "Conversation with Death," and David Mansfield, who produced some of the tracks, is heard on fiddle, backing Iris Dement in "Pretty Saro."

The film is worth seeing, but the songs will endure, as they always have. The lyrics are not included in the CD but can be downloaded from the Vanguard Web site www.vanguardrecords.com.

Some of those lyrics have been in my head since I first read the child ballads as a teenager and then sought out recordings of "traditional music," as it was called. The words turned into waking dreams, scenes of places to which I have never been, but they were there, and still are. Barbara Allen, having been spurned at the tavern by Sweet William, turns away from him at his death-bed. But, in town, hearing the death bells ringing, she sings:

"Oh Mother, oh mother, make my bed
Make it long and narrow
Sweet William died for me today
I'll die for him tomorrow

And out of his grave grew a red, red rose
And out of hers, a briar."

Says Maggie Greenwald: "What I think a lot of people will find is that this music sounds unlike anything they've heard before. Yet, at the same time it gives you a clear indication of where America pop and folk came from. And it affects the world at large. Kids listening to Bruce Springsteen in Prague, Moscow, and Beijing are really listening to the stuff that had its roots in Appalachia. And in England, Ireland, and Wales long before.

One night, many years ago, in Alan Lomax's loft in Greenwich Village, Jean Ritchie, the Clancy Brothers, and blues singers with roots in the Mississippi Delta filled the room and the street below with what the jubilant Lomax was calling the rivers of American music—the sources of which were far beyond our shores.

"American Routes"
Waters Roots of Folk

Louis Armstrong once said, "All music is folk music. Horses don't sing." In the history of American radio, no series has ever come close to Nick Spitzer's "American Routes" in exploring the many streams of this nation's music.

Heard via Public Radio International on more than 150 stations (visit www.amroutes.com for complete listings), the weekly two-hour series ranges from Cajun to country, from blues chants and klezmer rhythms to a New York cab driver singing of his old country, Transylvania. Also, gospel shouts and the Rebirth Brass Band of New Orleans, along with the Grateful Dead and Bob Dylan.

Mr. Spitzer, who was Louisiana's first official folklorist and then a specialist at the Smithsonian's folk division, has produced "American Routes" since April 1998 in an old water-bottling plant in the French Quarter of New Orleans. (It's funded by the Corporation for Public Broadcasting, the National Endowment for the Arts, the Louisiana Endowment for the Humanities, and Community Coffee, a New Orleans coffee company.)

Academic folklorists tend to specialize in such genres as Appalachian ballads, bluegrass, or Native American culture and to hold to the conviction that these once "pure" forms have been so adulterated by fusion with other idioms, especially commercial music, that only a few saving remnants still exist. But Mr. Spitzer challenges this belief. He has traveled, recorded, and interviewed throughout the land. And he emphasizes that, from the beginning, as Americans and new immigrants of all kinds of backgrounds have moved to new places for work and a better life, "they have merged their music as they have mixed socially and culturally," often enriching one another in the process. Mr. Spitzer believes that "all these musics deserve to be heard together as part of an understanding of the broader American cultural experience."

Mr. Spitzer also issues a challenge to the way music is all too often programmed on radio. "Instead of segregating music genres into discrete, market-driven formats of different classes and ethnicities," he presents what Alan Lomax—the Johnny Appleseed of folk music collectors—calls "the rainbow of American music."

Years ago, in New York clubs, it was possible to hear the Clancy Brothers exulting in Irish drinking songs; Jean Ritchie recalling, through the centuries, English ballads; and Sonny Terry transforming his harmonica into a train hurtling through the night. They and other variously rooted performers appeared together at festivals. And on one glorious night in the 1960s, at a song-swapping session at Mr. Lomax's New York apartment, a jubilant gathering of singers and players from proudly distinct cultures not only traded songs but a degree of mutual indebtedness in their latter-day styles.

I hadn't felt as exhilarated by such a musical galli-maufry until I heard a number of Nick Spitzer's "American Routes" broadcasts.

In December, for example, Mr. Spitzer mined the sounds of New York City. Starting with Duke Ellington's version of "The Sidewalks of New York," Mr. Spitzer then presented Carolina Slim, recorded last year in Grand Central Terminal, singing "The Subway Blues" for his living. Slim told listeners he had come to New York many years before from South Carolina, "where I was made." From his always pertinent collection of recordings, Mr. Spitzer played the "Second Avenue Square Dance," featuring the legendary klezmer clarinet virtuoso, Dave Tarras, followed by Woody Guthrie singing "New York Town."

Threaded through the program were such nonpareil folk as Louis Armstrong ("There's a Boat Dat's Leavin' Soon for New York"), Tito Puente ("On Broadway"), the Boswell Sisters ("42nd St.") and Chicago bluesman Jimmy Reed ("Going to New York").

Mr. Spitzer's conversational narration revealed a remarkable intimacy with many of the city's neighborhoods. And, from what he claimed are more than 40,000 licensed New York cabbies speaking seventy-six different languages, he found not only the Transylvanian troubadour but also a mellifluous driver, lately arrived from the Dominican Republic.

The people Nick Spitzer records and interviews are, he wrote in *Southern Changes* magazine, "in migration in history, in real life and in our show. Things that pop culture has turned into static icons are freed and allowed to flow again. The music selections speak to each other and to listeners."

Alan Lomax noted, during an interview in the New Orleans *Times-Picayune,* that "back in the thirties and forties, most people didn't like indigenous music. They thought it was something ignorant people did because they didn't know any better. Today we've accepted this music but still haven't truly heard it. It lives in out-of-the-way places, and we still don't understand its mysteries. Nick is one of the people I'm proudest of because he spends most of his time in the field, looking people up, helping them."

In a 1998 "American Routes"—as he recalled in the journal *Louisiana Cultural Vistas*—Mr. Spitzer traveled along Route 66. "We talked to the Navajos about the history of the highway that came through their land and brought them both problems and progress. We played multiple versions of 'Get Your Kicks on Route 66,' along with Native American music and West-Texas-oilfield rhythm-and-blues forms. All of which, when mashed together, offers fresh commentary on the nature of westward travel in the paved-over, road-weary twentieth century."

Describing his vocation, Mr. Spitzer said: "My job is to find performers in the community, support them where they live, and try to let others hear them. How do we reconcile 'progress' with the notion of keeping some of our past for the future? My job is to water the roots." And on "American Routes," he is also creating living archives for future generations.

A GIFT OF AMERICA
TO THE WORLD

When Langston Hughes was in high school in a small Illinois town, his teacher told the class that a poet, above all, had to have "rhythm." So, as Hughes recalled in an interview recently heard again on National Public Radio, "I came to the conclusion that me being a Negro, that little boy must have some rhythm to give to a poem, and maybe that's why I was elected the class poet."

Hughes did bring the rhythms of blues and jazz into his poems, but being black has not always been synonymous with jazz and blues time. Paul Robeson, backed by the Count Basie band in *King Joe*, a recorded tribute to Joe Louis—though so powerfully compelling in other contexts—was invincibly wooden, even with the easefully swinging Basie rhythm section behind him.

Yet, through the long, vibrant history of black music—from field hollers, work songs, and gospel to the stunningly brilliant improvisations of Louis Armstrong and the soul-stirring storytelling of Ray Charles and Duke Ellington—the rhythms of black American life have indeed reverberated around the world.

In *Say It Loud! A Celebration of Black Music in America* (Rhino, available in stories and at www.rhino.com), the boxed six-CD set ranges from Scott Joplin to Armstrong, Charlie Parker, Muddy Waters, John Coltrane, Marvin Gaye, Grand Master Flash and the Furious Five, Howlin' Wolf, and Thelonious Monk. Since this music is an integral part of American history, there are also, briefly threaded through the music, the actual voices of Booker T. Washington, W.E.B. Du Bois, Martin Luther King Jr., Malcolm X, Harry Truman proposing antilynching legislation, and Jackie Robinson speaking on the eve of the 1949 World Series.

Moving along with the music is a seventy-two-page book with archival photographs and time lines. Consider 1929: The Brotherhood of Sleeping Car Porters is admitted to the American Federation of Labor, and on Broadway, Fats Waller and Andy Razaf's *Hot Chocolates* arrives, including Louis Armstrong singing "Ain't Misbehavin'."

One of the many indications of the converging streams flowing in and out of black music is a comment by Lamond Dozier, a songwriter for Motown rhythm-and-blues recordings: "I listened to a lot of country music by myself because country music had the best stories, earthy stories people live by and could identify with." And there, on the fourth disc of "Say It Loud!," is black country-music singer Charley Pride ("Is Anybody Goin' to San Antone").

Ike Turner, nurtured by the blues in Mississippi juke joints, provides etymological illumination: "They didn't call it a juke joint because there was music in there. They just call it [that] because it was just people in there juking

and slow dragging and dancing. Now, you walk into Star-
bucks and start dancing, they throw you out."

Among the reflectively knowledgeable essayists in the
accompanying book are Gerald Early, professor of modern
letters at Washington University in St. Louis, and Ingrid
Monson, the Quincy Jones professor of African American
Studies and Music at Harvard University. She writes of
the common practice, as in the 1950s, of white singers
"covering" original songs and recordings by black performers. Those versions "generally duplicated the entire
textures of the originals, toning down the intensity of the
rhythm and vocal styles."

The black singers who were involuntarily covered, Ms.
Monson notes, "had little basis for contesting this practice,
since many had forfeited their publishing rights in order
to receive a recording contract (something many labels
insisted upon)." In this respect, too, the story of black
music encompasses more than its timbres and rhythms.

In addition to still-well-known performers in this
bonanza of black music, such as Sarah Vaughan, Tina
Turner, Mahalia Jackson, Billie Holiday, and Charles Mingus (he shows his roots in "Wednesday Night Prayer
Meeting"), there are abiding pleasures from such groups
as the Mills Brothers, whom Rhino might consider assem-
bling in a boxed set of their own. Their "Tiger Rag" here
is the very definition of swinging.

Also worth more extensive availability are the infec-
tiously good-humored and rhythmically resourceful
Louis Jordan & His Tympany Five ("Saturday Night Fish
Fry"). Less enlivening is Paul Robeson's "Ol' Man River."

He doesn't swing on that one, either. But when I was a teenager, I saved up to see and hear him as Othello, and those spoken rhythms were seismic.

Ernest Hardy, another essayist in the book—and a film and music critic for the *LA Weekly*—writes of how the vividly variegated music in *Say It Loud!* shows the way these singers and players "speak to one another across time, across categories. Not just in a neat continuum of the music—this begat that, which begat that, which spun off from that—but in a real interplay of ideas and notions, politics and philosophies . . . until themes, phrases and riffs from one era or genre make contact with and comment upon or underscore (or challenge) the music from another era or genre."

Otis Redding's "Change Gonna Come" by Sam Cooke speaks to The Neville Brothers' "Sister Rosa" ("We don't ride in the back of the bus no more"). And Louis Armstrong's exhilarating horn and scat singing on "Heebie Jeebies" reaches over time to Charlie Parker and Dizzy Gillespie's "Ko Ko." Pulsing through all the genres here—including some of the latter-day rap and hip hop that normally elude my definition of music—is the insistent life force of these sounds.

What also stays in my mind in all of this celebration is the voice of a man about to be killed. Following Diana Ross & The Supremes ("Love Child") is Martin Luther King Jr., speaking in Memphis to the black sanitation workers on strike: "Longevity has its place, but I'm not concerned about that now." Immediately after, on the same track, is a report of his assassination the next day.

There is a five-part television documentary of *Say It Loud!,* initiated by Quincy Jones, which has been shown twice on VH1, most recently during Black History Month. But these Rhino CDs and the forthcoming documentary version on VHF and DVD should be in each and every one of the nation's schools—a vital teaching tool in America's history classes.

JAZZ AHEAD

End of Jazz:
Hold That Note

I n the emerging days of bebop (later conventionally
called modern jazz), Dave Kapp, an influential producer at Decca Records, was alarmed by those careen-
ing new sounds and rhythms. He indignantly placed a sign
on his desk: "Where's the melody?"

Kapp's anxiety soon proved largely groundless. The two
icons of the new frontier turned out to be inventively
devoted to deeply melodic improvisation. Currently available, for instance, are Charlie Parker's "I'll Walk Alone"
(on *Charlie Parker at Storyville*, Blue Note) and Dizzy
Gillespie's "I Can't Get Started" (on *Dizzy in South America*, Volume 1, Red Anchor Productions, 1–800–425–6557).

However, according to a grim foretelling of the end of
jazz in the April 14 Wall Street Journal by Eric Felten ("All
Jazzed Up With Nowhere to Go"), "in jazz, melody has
been abandoned. . . . Without it, jazz may soon be reduced
to little more than murmuring mood music for a lazy
afternoon's canoodling."

I tried to decipher Mr. Felten's meaning of melody during a recent evening at St. Peter's Church in New York,
where a Duke Ellington theater work, "Renaissance Man,"

was being performed. The most penetrating solos were by Joe Lovano, a reigning modern-jazz tenor saxophonist, whose passionate, romantic balladry evoked the memory of Duke Ellington Orchestra alumnus Ben Webster. Lovano can be heard at length on *52nd Street Themes* (Blue Note).

A few nights later, at the City Hall restaurant in Manhattan, the large room abounded with the soaring, insistent melodies of the late Charles Mingus, as performed by the Mingus Orchestra. Its predominantly young members include a tenor saxophonist, Eli Digibri, recently arrived from Israel, and bassist Boris Kozlov, who first awakened to jazz in Russia. Both, while telling their own stories, fulfill—as do their colleagues—the intentions of Mingus, who, with Ellington, was the most enduring melodist in the history of jazz.

Lest readers of Mr. Felten's piece think I am citing only exceptions to his jeremiad about the death of melody in jazz, here is a partial list of releases within the past few months in which even someone new to jazz would easily find the melodies.

In *The Invisible Hand* (Blue Note), leader Greg Osby, an alto saxophonist and clarinetist and one of the more influential innovators in jazz, is joined by guitarist Jim Hall, whose career spans the entire history of modern jazz. Their devotion to melody is so lyrical that I expect this CD will be accompanying a goodly number of "lazy afternoon's canoodlings."

Also on Blue Note is *Nature Boy*, a panoply of such standards as "What Is This Thing Called Love?" and "Smoke Gets in Your Eyes." Alto saxophonist Jackie

McLean, the leader, was a disciple of Charlie "Bird" Parker, who insisted the youngster develop his own voice—which the young man triumphantly did.

As this set demonstrates, McLean has never abandoned melody. The composers of the songs he illuminates could not charge him with abuse of their intentions. McLean also teaches at the Hartt School of Music at the University of Hartford, and is developing players who can nurture a melodic line.

Charles McPherson is an alumnus of Charles Mingus's various jazz workshops—which were as challenging to the musicians involved as their continual surprises were to listeners. He has become a magisterial interpreter of melodies that I would think even Mr. Felten would have no difficulty recognizing. On *Manhattan Nocturne* (Arabesque Recordings), the full-voiced alto saxophonist personalizes "You're My Thrill" and "How Deep is the Ocean?" McPherson's credo is: "I want it all, the virtuosity mixed with heart." And as for his musicians' rhythmic sense, "I prefer dancing with someone who's flowing."

And then there is Marian McPartland. I first heard her in the mid-1950s at the Hickory House, a large restaurant in midtown Manhattan, where the musicians sat above a long bar where drinks were constantly mixed and dispensed. She had come here from England, and her sprightly, swinging trio, often stretching out on standards, cut through the conversations in the room.

On his very few nights off in New York, Duke Ellington would dine at Hickory House. One evening, her set ended, Marian came off the stand above the bar, looking expectantly at Ellington for any trace of approval.

Duke, ever gracious, gave her a regal smile and said, "My, you play so many notes." Years later, Marian told me, "I was green as grass then. It took me a while to realize what he was actually saying." Or, as Dizzy Gillespie once told me, "It took me all my life to learn what notes not to play."

In September 1998, at the new Birdland in Manhattan, the original Marian McPartland Hickory House Trio was reunited. The bassist was and is Bill Crow, who has also written engagingly about his life in jazz in *Jazz Anecdotes* (Oxford University Press). And Joe Morello, subtly attentive to swinging dynamics in the tradition of Big Sid Catlett, is on drums.

McPartland—born in Windsor, England, in 1920—continues to be as vital a part of the jazz scene as if she had been born in Chicago. She does so not only as a performer, but through her long-running Piano Jazz series on National Public Radio.

The buoyant reunion, Marian McPartland's *Hickory House Trio/Reprise* (Concord Jazz), recorded live, brought me back to my youth and theirs. As Bill Crow says in the notes, "The music came flooding back to us." And again I could see Duke, listening to "Street of Dreams," "Two for the Road" and Mercer Ellington's "Things Ain't What They Used to Be." But things *were* a lot as they used to be. The notes were fewer, but the melodies were as glowing as ever.

Sonny LaRosa's
Elementary School Jazz

Ever since I started writing about jazz, I've heard the recurring—and baseless—obbligato that jazz will soon be on life support. However, there is always the need to nurture new audiences, and players. Accordingly, the most exemplary project of Jazz at Lincoln Center is the Essentially Ellington High School Jazz Band Competition, now in its seventh year and newly extended to Australia with Essentially Ellington Down Under. Wynton Marsalis should take note that among these student instrumentalists challenged by Duke's scores there are many very proficient young women. Maybe Wynton will eventually offer one of them a chair in his male ensemble.

But with regard to the future of jazz, there is one solo educator—without any of the organizational and financial resources of Jazz at Lincoln Center—who deserves much more attention, and emulation. Sonny LaRosa, formerly a trumpet player with Sam Donahue, among others, is the director, arranger, and nurturer of America's Youngest Jazz Band. It's a big band and the players are from six to twelve years old. The band has existed for twenty-three years, but I first heard them last year at a four-day, annual March of Jazz party in Clearwater Beach, Florida, celebrating the seventy-fourth birthday of stubbornly youthful Ruby Braff.

The kids hit at nine in the morning, before some of the late-night revelers were ready for more. And as I also thought, "How much can kids say on their horns? Or swing?" But I was curious. As I later wrote in *The Wall Street Journal*, I was jolted by the band's impact in its opener, "Bugle Call Rag." This was jubilant, foot-tapping swinging. As the set went on, I noted, "They not only knew how to swing collectively, but the soloists could tell a story. A story limited by their brief experience in music and life but nonetheless theirs."

America's Youngest Jazz Band has joyously surprised other listeners at the Montreux Jazz Festival in Switzerland, various American festivals, and was probably the youngest band to perform at Preservation Hall in New Orleans during the New Orleans Jazz and Heritage Festival. For reasons I cannot understand, it has yet to be invited to play, of all places, at the annual assembly of International Association for Jazz Education, nor has George Wein ever invited the band to play at any of his festivals.

Writing the liner notes for the band's newest CD, *Live at March of Jazz 2002*, I quoted from *St. Petersburg Times* reporter Lane DeGregory's explanation of how Sonny LaRosa brings along his lively jazz apprentices: "Sonny arranges all the songs himself. He writes each part out by hand, for every instrument, individualizing the approach to each musician's ability (or lack thereof). He draws the notes in black marker. The fingerings beneath, in red. And he pencils the chord names in on top. He knows which kids can hold a long low C and who can hit a high F. He knows whose arms have grown enough to extend a trombone slide and who still needs help counting."

I remember, years ago, Duke Ellington telling me why the scores in his orchestra were not headed "first trumpet," "second trombone," and so on. Instead they usually had the names of each player. "I know the strengths and weaknesses of these musicians," Duke said, "and I write with that information in mind." But later, he told me, somewhat ruefully, "Now the younger ones coming into the band can play anything."

So will Sonny LaRosa's alumni. As the March 1999 *Mississippi Rag* reported: "It takes about two years of lessons to break in a new band member. Some who stay in the band until retirement at age thirteen often beg to stay 'just one more year.' The twelve-year-old limit is imposed to keep the band as young as possible."

Sonny is a vigorous seventy-six, and I think these kids keep him that way. David Liebman, a player of first-class musicianship, says: "Sonny LaRosa should be given the Medal of Freedom. Not only has he taught them each on their own instruments, but he has molded them into a truly remarkable unit. When you see the pride that is reflected in these youngsters' faces and the way they stand tall to strut their stuff—this gives you hope for the future of culture and the arts in this country." And, of course, the future of jazz.

I write this in the hope that other veterans of big bands will devote themselves to this fruitful way to keep the music alive. I can still see and hear these kids swinging into "One O'Clock Jump"—in their red jackets, black pants, white shirts, and bow ties, flourishing their instruments from side to side like the bands of my youth in the stage shows between movies. These youngsters are not playing at jazz, they herald the jazz to come. For information about the band's CDs and how to book the band. Sonny LaRosa is at 1129 Pelican Place, Safety Harbor, FL 34695. Phone: 727-725-1788; www.sonnylarosa.com; e-mail: sonny@sonnylarosa.com.

When I was a fourteen-year-old clarinetist, Ruby Braff, a year younger, invited me to a session at his home. As soon as he began to play, I gave up fantasizing I'd ever be on the road with anybody. But maybe, if a Sonny LaRosa had been there. . . .

CUTTING DOWN SOLOS TO
GET TO THE CUTTING EDGE

I never miss a Ben Ratliff piece in the *New York Times*, so that I can get a sense of the newer frontiers of jazz. And I've called him to get the phone number of a record label I'd never heard of. But in reaching for the cutting edge of jazz, the explorer can fumble and strike at the soul of jazz.

In a still reverberating article in the May 28, 2000, *New York Times*, "The Solo Retreats from the Spotlight in Jazz," Ratliff approvingly quoted Wynton Marsalis (via *JazzTimes*) on the future of jazz: "I think there will be more emphasis put on presentation and composition as opposed to just soloing, which is really a boring and predictable way of presenting music."

Marsalis was an unfortunate choice to bolster Ratliff's thesis because as an original soloist, Marsalis is not on the level of Bobby Hackett or Frankie Newton; and in the present, he's certainly not in the same league as Ruby Braff or Dave Douglas.

According to Ratliff, not only is the "blowing date" recording and its counterpart in live performance "more passé than ever," but the way to the further growth and depth of jazz is when the band seems "to be improvising all together" or the music becomes "heavily arranged." Alas, Oscar Peterson must also be a relic of the springtime of the music, for on National Public Radio he says that "what keeps jazz going is the way this tune affects me this night, this moment."

Sidney Bechet, of course, was right. You can't hold back jazz, or any creative expression. Living in Paris for a time, I went to a series of concerts at which then young Pierre Boulez was illuminating the new languages and forms of classical music, and I'd leave each one exhilarated and curious for more. But I still didn't abandon Beethoven's last quartets.

Nor, in jazz, am I an inveterate traditionalist. I was in the studio, and wrote the notes, for Ornette Coleman's first session on Lester Koenig's Contemporary label. Ornette helped me a great deal with those notes because for me, that music was as challenging as a roller coaster ride. And I have never ceased to be surprised at the uncategorizable wit and free spirit of Carla Bley. But the notion of the future of jazz as a series of planned surprises, with carefully limited space for solos, will indeed turn jazz into a lacquered "art form."

In a letter published in the June 11 *New York Times*, Keith Jarrett brought considerable light to Ratliff's dense vision of jazz's liberation from its retrograde fixation on solos. Wrote Jarrett: "The spirit of jazz is the spirit of personal freedom. There is no literature, no repertory of personal freedom, only spontaneous individual acts. Jazz needs these acts of freedom to reconfirm itself in every era. It is in the player's art, not the writer's. There is no future if there is no present."

This is not to say that Duke Ellington did not embody the spirit of personal freedom. But as he often told me, he focused on the personal spirit—including the improvisatory identity—of each musician. And that was why when a player new to the orchestra would ask Duke what he was supposed to play in a forthcoming solo, Duke would answer: "Listen, sweetie, listen." Not only listen to the vibrant context that Ellington had set, but to what the score ignited within the soloist. Moreover, all the written parts were marked specifically for each player. And Duke once reprimanded a new trombonist for playing a solo like Lawrence Brown on a number previously identified with Brown.

As skillfully as the Lincoln Center Jazz Orchestra recreates Ellington under Wynton Marsalis, will any of those performances, including the solos, endure as the originals have and will? Are Ben Webster, Johnny Hodges, and Rex Stewart passé as soloists in the most incandescent body of compositions yet in jazz history?

The closest compositional accomplishment to Ellington's—and, I think, in many ways equal—was that of Charles Mingus. He was hardly miserly in the space he gave to soloists, and he would rail at them stingingly in public if their solos did not tell who each of them was "this night, this moment!"

In my time as an A&R man for Candid Records, there were some dates with a lot of paper. And there were times when the players got stuck, as on flypaper. My usual role was only to select the leader who would choose the side-men and be in charge of the final cut. My job was also to send out for sandwiches and keep the engineer from being too technologically "inventive." But when the music got tangled in the scores, I would leave the control room and would suggest—I never had the nerve to mandate—that maybe they might play some blues. The paper jam broke, and that passe "blowing session" lasted quite a while to the evident pleasure and relief of the players. And later, the manuscript paper came alive, too.

There is no future, as Keith Jarrett says, if there is no present. And, as T.S. Eliot said, there is no future if there is no present and no past.

History Lessons
Via Jazz

Charles Black was a key member of Thurgood Marshall's team of lawyers during its long march to the Supreme Court's decision in *Brown v. Board of Education* that declared racially segregated public schools unconstitutional. Later, Black, then a Yale law professor, wrote in the *Yale Law Journal* how he, a white Texan who grew up racist, had an experience that eventually brought him to Thurgood Marshall.

In 1931, the sixteen-year-old future lawyer heard Louis Armstrong at a hotel in Austin. "He was the first genius I had ever seen," Black wrote. "It is impossible to overstate the significance of a sixteen-year-old southern boy's seeing genius, for the first time, in a black. We literally never saw a black then in any but a servant's capacity."

"It was just then," he continued, "that I started walking toward the Brown case where I belonged." And that Louis Armstrong became part of American constitutional history.

Less dramatically, Ken Burns told the New York Times that in first researching his nineteen-hour documentary "Jazz," he had only a marginal knowledge of the lives of the

musicians. But he found that "on every level—mythologi-
cal, sensual, political, and social—jazz informed me about
who we are as a people. I didn't expect to learn so much."

Part of an American Time Line

Having listened through the years to the life stories of
scores of jazz musicians—from Sidney Bechet to John
Coltrane—I've often wished that jazz could be taught as
part of a continuing time line of American history. Now,
for the first time, in the public schools of Sarasota
County, Florida, it is. Some 2,500 fifth-graders in twenty
elementary schools are learning American history to the
accompaniment of the experiences and the sounds of the
makers of jazz. The students are being told, for example,
about the "field hollers" of slaves that carried from one
plantation to another in violation of the law forbidding
such communication—giving birth to the blues.

The program is called "JazzLinks: Jazz Connects to
History" and was created by the Jazz Club of Sarasota.
The idea originated with Lucy White, now eighty-three,
who, while living as a student in Harlem during the
1930s, heard such now-legendary figures as Duke Ellington, Louis Armstrong, Chick Webb, and Billie Holiday at
the Apollo Theater and Savoy Ballroom.

In Florida, Ms. White, a board member of the Jazz Club
of Sarasota, spent fifteen years bringing local musicians
into the schools; but, she told me, "only a small portion
of the kids were being reached. I wanted every child to

know this important contribution to our history. I'm black, but I didn't want this to be part only of black history, separated from the rest of the American story. This way too, jazz will keep going through the generations. Otherwise, it will fade away."

Under the direction of the jazz club's Nancy Roucher and a team of experts in art, music, and history, including the authoritative historian Carroll Buchanon, the county's fifth-grade teachers receive kits that include videotapes, art and photo reproductions, books, CDs (especially the invaluable *Smithsonian Collection of Classic Jazz* by Martin Williams), teacher manuals and student workbooks.

JazzLinks is taught simultaneously in both the regular fifth-grade classrooms and the music classrooms. There are ten social-studies lessons. One of them, as described by the team, "traces the great migration of African-Americans from the South to the North through the art of Jacob Lawrence and the development of 'urban' jazz." In the music classes, there are eight lessons illustrating the distinctive styles of players and composers while also enabling students to compose and perform the common language of jazz—the blues. At the end of each unit, jazz musicians come in to illustrate the styles covered in the lesson, and are interviewed by the students.

Music Brings It All Together

In the jazz club's publication, *Sarasota Jazz Sounds*, Denise Roberts, managing director of the Venice Foundation, which provided the source money for the program, says: "I have performed dozens of follow-up visits in the public schools and have never seen children so engaged by a program. The material the teachers were trying to get across was totally alien to these kids. The Jim Crow laws might as well have been in place centuries ago instead of just decades ago as far as these kids knew, but the music brought it all together for them."

And Fran Valencic, a fifth-grade teacher at the Taylor Ranch School in Venice, Florida, reports: "As a classroom teacher, I learned so much I didn't realize about our history. My students and I also came to love the music. Some of the boys and girls decided to form small jazz bands of their own. Every student in this class was either in the band or in the chorus."

In his autobiography, *Treat It Gentle* (Da Capo Press), Sidney Bechet tells of his grandfather Omar, a slave who on Sundays would gather with other slaves in New Orleans's Congo Square. Omar "made his own drums out of skins of a pig or a horse hide. And he knew horns." He told his grandson of the dreams he and other slaves had at night: "Things would come to them out of Africa, things they'd heard about or had seen. And in all that recollecting, somehow there wasn't any of it that didn't have part of a music-form in it."

Bechet, the most powerful of all jazz wind players, wrote his life story because he felt that most people didn't understand how this music "made the Negro feel he can mean something" despite Jim Crow in all its forms and disguises. His book would make an illuminating addition to the curriculum in the Sarasota schools.

As news of the enlightened fifth-graders there spreads, other school systems around the country are asking the Jazz Club of Sarasota how they can create their own JazzLinks. "I feel," says Ms. White, "that JazzLinks is the single most important program that we have in the jazz club." And beyond. Lucy White too has become a force in American history.

TOSHIKO AKIYOSHI:
RISING FROM THE ABYSS

I n the early 1950s, jazz impresario Norman Granz,
returning from a concert tour of Japan, told me of a
recording he had made in Tokyo of a twenty-three-
year-old pianist, Toshiko Akiyoshi. Oscar Peterson had
heard her in a coffee shop and alerted Granz.

When she came to Boston in 1956 to study at the
Berklee School of Music, I heard Toshiko often. Because
she was a fluently secure melodic swinger, more experienced jazzmen welcomed her on gigs. Immersed in jazz
since she was a teenager, her dream of being where it all
started, she told me, had come true.

In the early 1960s, she co-led a combo with her then-
husband, alto saxophonist Charlie Mariano, and I
recorded her during my short tenure as an A&R man for
Candid Records. Jazz was her natural language.

Toshiko went on to the demanding graduate school of
Charles Mingus's orchestra; and no longer married to
Charlie Mariano, she formed an enduring musical and life
partnership with the unaccountably underrated tenor
saxophonist and flutist Lew Tabackin. A self-challenger,
like Toshiko, he too never stops evolving. In Los Angeles

in 1973, she formed with him an intriguing orchestra that celebrated its thirtieth anniversary at a Carnegie Hall concert.

During all those years, Toshiko had never thought about interweaving Japanese music with her jazz life. What persuaded her to learn more about her roots was—to my surprise when she said this in a July 2003 *Down Beat* interview—an article I had written in the *Village Voice* when Duke Ellington died. He had often told me that what drove him as a composer and orchestra leader was to tell the history of his people in America, embedded in the black musical and life experiences of the centuries that preceded him.

"Reading that triggered me," she told Michael Bourne in *Down Beat.* "I thought that should be my job—to employ some of my heritage, to put Japanese culture into jazz."

In a number of her compositions—such as "Drum Conference," commissioned by, and performed at, Jazz at Lincoln Center this year—she has been doing that job with characteristically singular inventiveness and a sure sense of textural dynamics that make her orchestra the most subtly dramatic in present-day jazz.

The climax so far of Toshiko's bringing her heritage into her jazz life is *Hiroshima—Rising from the Abyss.* First performed, and recorded, at Hiroshima on August 24, 2001, it has now been released in this country on the True Life label (available at Amazon.com and many record stores).

As she told me, Toshiko had never thought of writing music about the horrifying devastation inflicted on the people of Hiroshima by this country on August 6, 1945, when she was fifteen. "But at that time," she told writer Michael Bourne, "people tried to avoid talking about it. Even the victims." In 1999, however, a Buddhist priest, Nakagawa, asked her to write music memorializing that fateful date in his hometown. He sent her photographs taken three days after the bomb. In her notes to the American release of *Beyond the Abyss,* she writes that the pictures were so horrifying that she couldn't imagine what music she could bring to them.

"But," Toshiko continues, "one photo caught my eye. It was a young woman who came out of a bomb shelter looking at the sky, smiling a little with beautiful eyes full of hope." Seeing those eyes convinced Toshiko she could find in herself the music to honor, among the others, that young woman. Toshiko quotes the Dalai Lama: "We human beings cannot live without hope."

On the True Life CD, "From the Abyss" is the centerpiece. There are three sections of this memorial work: "Futility-Tragedy," "Survivor Tales," and "Hope." The entire set's first track, before the main composition, is "Long Yellow Road," and the last track, "Wishing Peace," has so moving a flute solo by Lew Tabackin that, Toshiko tells me, "tears come to my eyes when we perform it."

The most haunting, deeply reverberating section, "Survivor Tales," has a Hiroshima high-school student, Ryoko Shigemori, reading from an eyewitness account of the deaths and disfigurements, the "Mother's Diaries" from the Hiroshima Memorial Museum. Along with the reader, commenting on these tales is Wong Jang-Hyun, a master of traditional Korean flute.

The high-school student reads: "There was a rumor we would not have vegetation for seventy-five years. . . . But here, trees are growing, grass is greener than ever. . . . This is our message to the world from Hiroshima. . . . No nuclear and atomic weapons, and peace on earth."

The thirtieth anniversary concert of Toshiko Aki-yoshi's orchestra on October 17 at Carnegie Hall will include a performance of "Beyond the Abyss" with Wong Jang-Hyun, together with masters of traditional Japanese drums. It will be the orchestra's final appearance. "I'm seventy-three now," Toshiko told me. "I started as a pianist, and I believe I can play better, that I can improve myself. So I will go back to the piano with a small group."

Over half a century, Toshiko, in her music and in her life, has exemplified the resilient life force of jazz, and of the message of hope from Hiroshima in "Survivor Tales."

THE NEWEST JAZZ GENERATION

Although I have tentatively been converted to jazz-with-computers—but only so far as passionately exemplified by Dave Douglas on *Freak In* (RCA/Bluebird)—I am much more firmly encouraged about the future of jazz because of the frontiers Howard Bankhead is conquering through the Tennessee Valley Jazz Society. His Jazz Education in the Schools should become a model for the rest of the country.

Bankhead was born in Florence, Alabama, the hometown of W.C. Handy, and attended an elementary school named for that herald of the blues. For twenty-one years, he has been evangelizing for jazz in the schools of Tennessee Valley (lower middle Tennessee and all of North Alabama). Last year, for example, he brought live jazz and its history for free to more than fifteen schools in Huntsville/Madison County.

He focuses primarily on kindergarten through the eighth grade. A few years ago, in New York, I apprehensively brought some recordings of a George Lewis New Orleans band and Duke Ellington to a fourth-grade class. Could kids that young dig this? They wound up dancing to the music, and their teacher joined in. Howard Bankhead has brought that same joy of jazz to thousands of kids.

Bankhead is black, and during his programs in Black History Month, along with the rest of the school year, he notes, "Black history is for black kids, polka-dot kids, green kids, white kids, all kinds of kids. This music is for everyone." During any given month, he begins by exposing all the students in a school to live jazz. At the Ed White Middle School in Huntsville, fourteen-year-old eighth-grader Tori Tyler plays French horn, trumpet and some piano, but until the Bankhead troupe came, she hadn't heard or played any jazz. "Now," she says, "I'd like to play some of this. It's different from what I hear every day."

The schoolchildren learn the history of the music together with the sounds and the beat. As Bankhead says, "Jazz history is American history." Fifth-graders throughout the public schools of Sarasota, Florida, are also learning that lively lesson in their American history classes through the impetus of the Sarasota Jazz Society. There's been some interest in that combination from other school systems.

In the Tennessee Valley, the youngsters are also learning the connection between jazz and math. *The Huntsville Times* covered a visit by the Tennessee Valley Jazz Society to the Martin Luther King Jr. Elementary School. On trumpet, Jothan Callins, a real pro from Birmingham, was playing songs by Thelonious Monk and Erskine Hawkins. Second-grader Deomica Ussery was waving her arms, directing the show from her seat.

Buoyed by the audience's enthusiasm, Callins stopped for a quick math lesson.

"You've got to be able to count to play music," he said, as he showed them how to clap in three-four time during a section of "Tuxedo Junction." Not all the kids found the groove, but it gave math a new dimension. Talking to them about improvisation, Callins said: "Everybody gets to play. It's like being at church and having testimony time. We all get a chance to say our piece."

Sitting toward the back, *The Huntsville Times* reported, the principal, John W. Humphrey, was clapping to the music along with the kids. "For our African-American students," he said, "this gives them knowledge that they have a heritage to be proud of. And on a musical level, it's good just letting them get a close look at these instruments that they haven't seen before." But Bankhead also spreads the word that all the kids discover an American heritage of which they can be proud. Some of the youngsters have been moved to find their own instruments, to say their piece.

Howard Bankhead has a skill much needed in jazz for all ages. A resourceful promoter, he has linked his Tennessee Valley Jazz Society with Alabama A&M University's Telecommunications Center and the state's Arts Council. He also conducts summer jazz clinics, jazz workshops and the annual "Jazz-N-June" as part of the Mountain Jazz and Music Festival, one of Alabama's oldest and most popular music festivals.

For Bankhead's 2003 Jazz & Black History Celebration, Randy Weston—the master educator, pianist, and composer—will be the headliner. "This work," Bankhead told me, "is designed to develop the youth to be receptive to jazz and a broader vision of culture. We must do it early in their lives before Wall Street and pop culture capture them and their imagination."

It's a pity National Public Radio has no room for the reverberating outreach of the Tennessee Valley Jazz Society. But the ever-determined Bankhead keeps writing grant proposals, and perhaps the National Endowment for the Arts will understand that what he is generating could nourish the rest of the country. (IAJE can learn from him, too.) Bankhead can be reached at: 256-858-0409 or tvjs@aol.com.

CATEGORIZING THE
FUTURE OF JAZZ

The pungent cornetist Muggsy Spanier, who found his life's vocation by listening as a youth to Louis Armstrong, once punched critic Leonard Feather— an advocate of modern jazz—in the chops a half-century or so ago during the war between the "moldy figs" and the beboppers. Muggsy resented being consigned to a museum.

I thought of that civil war when reading an article by Brian Gilmore in the December 2002 issue of *The Progressive* in which he quoted Reuben Jackson, the Smithsonian Institution's Ellington archivist, declaring jazz to be "moribund." My dictionary's definition of moribund: "having little or no vital force left." Gilmore, however, believes that "free jazz" will rescue the music from its doldrums and jazz may even become political again, as it was in the 1960 and 1970, when, he writes, it "thundered about injustice."

That analysis of much of the present state of the music was in my mind when I went to the Blue Note in New York on December 9, 2002, for its twenty-first anniversary celebration, honoring eighty-two-year-old Clark Terry. Having spent most of my time in recent months trying to wrest the Bill of Rights back from John Ashcroft, I was beat. But once Clark—having thanked those present for their support during his "siege with cancer"—started to play, the life force of the music lifted me up, as it always has.

Clark, even more inventive than when I used to hear him with Duke Ellington and Count Basie, was jubilantly swinging, along with then eighty-year-old Frank Wess, seventy-six-year-old Jimmy Heath and alto saxophonist Dave Glasser, a mere forty years old. On drums, sounding like the fiery incarnation of Art Blakey, Sylvia Cuenca, in her thirties, was in total, resourceful command of her instrument, trading wit-laced breaks with Clark and driving the horns and the rest of us into a joyousness beyond categories and politics—even the present Orwellian actualization of *1984* in real time under Ashcroft. Speaking of his incandescent drummer later, Clark told me, "She sat in with my band ten years ago and I never wanted her to leave." I doubt if he asked Sylvia her politics.

A few days later, I met Jim Hall on the street where we both live. He was walking his dog, Django, and I had Lulu (named after "Lulu's Back in Town"). I asked the seventy-two-year-old guitarist and composer whether he feels jazz is "moribund." He laughed. "Except for the museum mentally of Wynton Marsalis," Jim said, "how can it be? The spirit of this music ain't going to die unless the world blows up." Hall, who never stops growing musically, can and does play with ease and authority with musicians of all styles and ages. "I've played," he said, "what we call jazz with people all over the world with whom I couldn't have a conversation. It's humans listening to each other, across barriers. The music isn't moribund. Whoever said that should get out more."

In the January/February issue of *JazzTimes*, Stuart Nicholson, who has communicated a lot about the music to listeners, wrote about Matthew Shipp's *Equilibrium* and said it "moves beyond the so-called 'jazz tradition' to the real jazz tradition . . . inspired by the present and future as much (or more) than the past." As Sidney Bechet wrote in his autobiography, *Treat It Gentle*, you can't hold the music back, but Charlie Parker, a master of the blues, was inspired *as much* by the past as by what he was creating that shaped the future of the music.

I remember Bird telling me with passion of having listened again to Bartók's "Second Piano Concerto." He said, "I heard things in it I never heard before. You never know what's going to happen when you listen to music. All kinds of things can suddenly open up"—as happened to me listening to Clark Terry at the Blue Note. On the way home, I bought *The Complete Beethoven String Quartets* by the Alban Berg Quartet, and again there were the quickening surprises that also come whenever I hear Louis Armstrong's "West End Blues."

On a new recording by trombonist-composer David Manson, *Fluid Motion* (isospinlabs.com), I heard, for the first time, twenty-year-old trumpeter Jonathon Powell. Powell's crackling range and the electricity of his imagination reminded me of the first time I heard Lee Morgan and Clifford Brown. I didn't think of Jonathon Power as a category. His voice is his own, as is that of the always-contemporary seventy-nine-year-old Sam Rivers, on the same date.

Duke Ellington used to say, "I don't want people analyzing my music, putting it into categories. Just listen!" Jimmy Giuffre, speaking of John Coltrane, said, "I began to understand that his statements on his horn were as if he was standing naked on the stage—the music coming directly from the man, not the horn." This is the real tradition in all music that lasts—what David Murray calls "the signature sound." Duke Ellington once said to me: "The other night I heard a cat on the radio talking about 'modern' jazz and playing a record to illustrate his point, but it had devices I heard cats using in the 1920s. These large words like 'modern' don't mean anything. Everybody who's had anything to say in this music—all the way back—has been an individualist."

So long as there are true uncategorizable individualists, jazz can never be moribund.

LAST CHORUS

THE LION, FATS, AND
MY OTHER MENTORS

When I heard, to my great surprise, that the National Endowment for the Arts had designated me, a non-musician, as the first writer on jazz to be one of its annual "Jazz Masters in 2004," I began to think of my debt to these musicians who have been a necessary, nurturing part of my life since I was eleven years old.

There was Willie, "the Lion" Smith, a master of the joyous, endlessly melodic school of Harlem stride piano. He had been a mentor of Duke Ellington, who spoke of "the luxury of the Lion's fire, his harmonic lavishness, his stride." As the grandmaster of stride piano, James P. Johnson, said: "When Willie Smith walked into a place, his every move was a picture."

Soon after I became New York editor of *Down Beat* in 1953, the Lion—a nickname for his fighting prowess in an all-black First World War unit—decided to be my mentor in various matters, including multiculturalism. He spoke Yiddish and had been a cantor in a Harlem synagogue.

At the piano, sporting a derby and a jutting cigar, he exemplified James P. Johnson's description of orchestral Harlem piano: "full, round, big widespread chords and tenths—a heavy bass moving against the right hand." And with Willie, there was also, at times, a delicate, wistful lyricism.

In 1958, I recorded a solo set by the Lion and, on the same session for a West Coast label, a solo recital by another legendary "tickler," (as the striders were called), Luckey Roberts.

Now a CD, *Luckey & The Lion: Harlem Piano* (Good Time Jazz/Fantasy Records), is still in the Fantasy Records catalog, available on fantasyrecords.com.

In a historic video documentary by Marc Fields, *Willie the Lion: A musical biography*—released in 2002 by NJN Public Television, and broadcast by PBS (for future availability 609-777-5093)—I saw Duke Ellington's comment on the impact of the Lion on jazz piano: "The Lion was a myth you saw come alive." My life has been full of such jazz myths.

Another myth had been a pupil of James P. Johnson, and the Lion used to say of the apprentice, "Yeah, a yearling, he's coming along. I guess he'll do all right." The yearling, Thomas "Fats" Waller surely did. During the oddly named Great Depression, I was trolling on the radio for jazz remotes, and found The Panther Room in Chicago where the announcer, after describing the ornate surroundings, including the diners and drinkers, introduced the performer.

Coming to the microphone, Waller said: "I wonder what the poor folks are doing tonight." It was warming to know that he was thinking of me. Around that time, his music sent me to Boston's William Lloyd Garrison elementary school every morning because a local disc jockey always included in drive time Fats Waller's "Your Feet's Too Big." I came to school, chuckling.

When I was sixteen and a cub reporter for my college paper, the *Northeastern News*, Waller came to town. I was sure he'd never heard of Northeastern University, but I called him at his hotel and asked for an interview. He took me to dinner in the hotel, and told me of his "first love," the organ. He had taught young Bill (Count) Basie to play that instrument. In Paris, Fats said, the legendary organist Marcel Dupré had let him play the organ at the church of Saint Sulpice.

He told me he had wanted to record a series of classical organ works, but there was no market for that by a Harlem strider. Fats can be heard on Hammond electronic organ, piano, and vocals on a singular CD—one of many revelations produced by George H. Buck, Jr., a resourceful New Orleans jazz enthusiast whose Jazzology label, and other imprints, will be mined for classic jazz long into the future.

On George Buck's Solo Art label, he has resurrected, in *The Amazing Fats Waller: Then You'll Remember Me*, nearly an hour of 1939 transcriptions—prerecorded radio programs leased to independent radio stations. Fats's lifelong interest in the instrument, the notes say, started, when, accompanying his preacher father on Harlem street corners, he played the harmonium, a small reed organ.

The repertory ranges widely from spirituals, transmuted operatic excerpts, folk songs, and even "The Old Oaken Bucket." The 19th century spiritual, "Deep River," becomes a deeply private meditation: and "The harmful little harmful," as Fats used to be billed, emerges in a jumping celebration of "The Lord Delivered Daniel." (jazzology.com, 504 525 5000).

The vintage blues and "hot jazz" Fats Waller I heard from the Panther Room while my parents thought I was asleep, resounds on Naxos's *Fats Waller Vol. 2/The Original 1939 Transcriptions* (naxos.com). These were transcribed, actually in 1938, when he was broadcasting from New York's Yacht Club.

With his regular small combo, including Gene "Honey Bear" Sedric on clarinet and tenor saxophone—from his own "Honeysuckle Rose," "Ain't Misbehavin'" and the rollicking strike of "Handful of Keys" to a spaciously romantic solo on "Poor Butterfly"—the man who had sent me to school each morning in such good humor brought to mind Louis Armstrong's toast:

"Fats is gone now . . . but to me, he's still here with us . . . Right now, every time someone mentions Fats Waller's name, why you can see the grin on all the faces . . .

Years ago, in my book, *Jazz Is*, now out of print, I wrote of Fats and my other jazz mentors: "As a boy, they seemed to me a different species. I could ask a ball player or a movie star for an autograph, but I was speechless when Johnny Hodges or Lester Young walked by on the way to a gig in Boston. I was in awe of jazz musicians because of the mystery of their overwhelming power . . .

"Nothing else in my experience was so exhilarating, so utterly compelling. The laughter in the music, the intimacy, the range and bite of life-tales each player told in textures and cadences entirely his own. The irony, the deep blues, and, as I grew older, the sensuousness.

"Once you're inside the music you'll want to keep going deeper and deeper, because it is impossible to get enough of it."

A while ago, a very young tenor saxophonist asked me, "Did you actually, *know*, talk to, Lester Young?" I told him how the mythical president of the tenor saxophone had asked me, "Do you like [white] Dixieland?" "If it's good," I said. Pres nodded, "Me too."

And the Lion said: "Music doesn't stem from any single race, creed, or locality. It comes from a mixture of all these things. As does the Lion."

LAST CHORUS

My introduction to "the rainbow of American music" happened when I was about five—the first music that made me run, literally, to hear more. The musicians were Yiddish-American klezmorim, who played for weddings at a catering hall (attached to a synagogue) a block from my home in Boston.

These were descendants of the itinerant Jewish bands that roamed through Eastern Europe—the Old Country—where my parents, grandparents, and their grandparents came from. The original klezmorim wandered through many cultures—when they weren't banished because they were Jewish—and they absorbed many of those sounds and rhythms as they passed through. The klezmorim were multiculturalists.

In the New World, the klezmorim were more than touched by jazz and more popular strains, but they retained their Jewish "soul." As soon as I heard their joyous, infectious dance music, I'd rush to the hall, and looking through the window, I'd marvel at, as I recalled in *Boston Boy*:

"The strutting trumpet player, bending and cracking his notes like he was eating nuts, winking at the bride and at any other girl up to ninety. The clarinetist, my hero, his notes dancing, making even the rebbe nod with a little smile; and playing with such a cry, a *krechts*, in a song that brought back all that Jews had gone through to be able to drink and dance in this place in America."

When I was in my teens, I'd still come running as I heard their musical cartwheels. The melodies like sunshowers, the rhythms that should have been bottled like seltzer. There was nothing else like it—except, by then, jazz.

"So, the klezmer clarinetist would say to me, "where do you think Benny Goodman came from?"

By then, I also had a sense of where the blues had come from. My own native blues. I'd come to know Joe Turner, Howlin' Wolf, Muddy Waters, and other black blues bards, and they, inadvertently, had brought me back to my childhood in an Orthodox *shul* (synagogue) where I heard other improvisers, the chazans!

One of the recurring images in this book:

In his black robes and high black skullcap, the chazan (the cantor) looms over the congregation. As the spirit comes, he closes his eyes, and speaks to God, with whom he also argues from time to time. What he sings is partly written but largely improvised. He is a master of melisma—for each sacred syllable, there are three, four, six notes that climb and entwine, throbbing in wait for the next spiraling cluster.

The chazan is a tenor, what they call in opera dramatic tenor, but what drama in opera is comparable to this continued dialogue with God? An atheist by the time I was thirteen, I nonetheless suspend my disbelief as I listen to these soaring—and sometimes chilling—conversations.

The cry. The *krechts* (a catch in the voice, a sob, a summoning of centuries of ghosts of Jews). The dynamics of the chazan are stunning—a thunderstorm of fierce yearning that reverberates throughout the *shul* as, in the balcony, the segregated women nod, and some moan, in anticipation and apprehension. God might answer.

Then, as if the universe has lost a beat, there is sudden silence. But no, there is a sound, a far distant sound, coming, my God, from deep inside the chazan—an intimation of falsetto, a sadness so unbearably compressed that I wonder the chazan does not explode. The room is swaying; the chazan, eyes still closed, does explode—his soul, riding a triumphant vibrato, goes right through the roof.

Years later, between sets at a bar in New York, I am telling a black nationalist and Charles Mingus, a citizen of the universe, about these Jewish blues—blues that are thousands of years old, diaspora blues even in America. The "soul music" of my youth, and then some.

Mingus is interested. He wants to hear some of my recordings of these trombones of God from the Old Country. But the black nationalist waves me and my blues away. There is only one color of the blues, he says. His. Mingus waves him away. Mingus says words sure get in the way of listening.

When I had a classical music program in Boston, I wouldn't name the composer or the performers until each recording was ended. That irritated many listeners because their preconceptions of particular composers, styles, or periods were shattered. They suddenly liked music they had been sure was cherished only by squares.

Also, on my jazz and folk music programs, I'd sometimes not say a categorizing word until each recording was over. More stereotypes were bruised. So were mine, about country music, when I was forced, on that radio station, to play an hour of those "hillbilly" sounds every day. (Boston and environs had a lot of listeners to country and Western music.) And so, Kitty Wells, Bob Wills, Hank Snow, and the stories they told led me later to Patsy Cline, Loretta Lynn ("The Coalminer's Daughter"), Merle Haggard, Willie Nelson, and other "hillbillies" who told me about lives and places that connected with my own life stories.

As I hope the storytellers in this book will connect with your memories and desires.

CREDITS

Many of the essays in this book originally appeared in other publications, sometimes under different titles, as indicated below.

The Jazz Voice

Billie Holiday: "The Ghosts of 'Strange Fruit'": *Jazz-Times*, October 2002

Billie Holiday: "Lady Day—All the Way": *Wall Street Journal*, March 5, 2002 as "The Frank and Tragic Voice of Lady Day"

Ivie Anderson: "For the Love of Ivie": *JazzTimes*, April 2001

Teddy Grace: "A Joyful Reunion with the Blues of Teddy Grace": *Wall Street Journal*, April 11, 1996

Abbey Lincoln: "God Bless the Child That Has Her Own": *New York Times*, March 3, 2002 as "Memories of an Unlikely Firebrand"

Frank Sinatra: "Sinatra in Paris with Small Combo": *Wall Street Journal*, January 19, 1995

Fred Astaire: "Some Singing—and Hoofing—with the Boys": *Wall Street Journal*, November 14, 2002

The Blues

"You Heard It Here First: When the Sun Goes Down": *Wall Street Journal*, October 31, 2002

Joe Williams: "He Brought the Blues from the Country to the City": *JazzTimes*, June 1999

"Jazz and Deep Jewish Blues": *JazzTimes*, January/February 2002

"The Everliving Blues": *JazzTimes*, December 1999

The Masters

Jo Jones: "The Man Who Played Like the Wind": *Jazz-Times*, November 2001

Johnny Hodges: "Life Could Be a Dream When He Blew Alto": *Wall Street Journal*, February 2, 2002

Charles Mingus: "Mingus Lives": *Wall Street Journal*, April 18, 1997

Charles Mingus: "The Incomplete History of Charles Mingus": *JazzTimes*, November 2000

Lester Young: "He Always Told a Story": *JazzTimes*, November 2000

Duke Ellington: "Duke Ellington's Mission": *Jazz-Times*, May 1999

Duke Ellington: "The Piano Player in the Band": *Wall Street Journal*, June 11, 1999

Duke Ellington: "Inside the Ellington Band": *Jazz-Times*, October 1999

Phil Woods: "The Irrepressible Spirit of Jazz": *Jazz-Times*, April 2002

Frankie Newton: "The Search for Frankie Newton": *JazzTimes*, November 2002

Cecil Taylor: "It's About Music and Capturing Spirits": *JazzTimes*, January/February 2002

Dizzy Gillespie: "Dizzy's Life Force Goes On": *Jazz-Times*, October 2001

Dick Wellstood: "Swinging at the Sticky Wicket": *Wall Street Journal*, June 5, 1988

Jack Teagarden: "Teagarden Time": *Wall Street Journal*, April 9, 1999

Carla Bley: "Carla Goes Her Own Way": *Wall Street Journal*, February 13, 2001

Wycliffe Gordon: "The Talking Trombone": *Wall Street Journal*, March 18, 2001

Louis Armstrong: "They Would Beat Jesus If He Was Black and Marched": *JazzTimes*, October 2000

Louis Armstrong: "Don't Let Anybody Tell You Louis Is Dead": *JazzTimes*, December 2003

Woody Herman: "Woody Herman's Down-Home Personal Blues": *Wall Street Journal*, August 22, 2001

Norman Granz: "Goodbye My Friend": *JazzTimes*, March 2002

John Coltrane: "The Spoken Essence": *JazzTimes*, September 2002

Dave McKenna: "King of the Two Hands": *Wall Street Journal* May 10, 2002

Ralph Ellison: "Literary Jazzman": *Wall Street Journal*, June 14, 2002

Clifford Brown: "A Trumpet as Sweet as His Sound": *Wall Street Journal*, February 15, 1996

Scott Robinson: "The Sound That Time Forgot": *Wall Street Journal*, August 4, 2000

Ruby Braff: "Horn Player Ruby Braff Was Anything But Old-Fashioned": *Wall Street Journal*, April 9, 2003

Ageless Big and Small Bands

"Jazz for Lunch at the Cajun": *JazzTimes*, September 2003

"Jubilant Sounds Swinging Through America": *Wall Street Journal*, June 18, 2003

"A Thrilling Big Jazz Band": *JazzTimes*, November 2003

The Business of Jazz

John Levy: "A Personal Manager Beyond Category": *JazzTimes*, September 2001

Art Davis: "The Mystery of Making It": *JazzTimes*, March 2001

"Musicians Taking Care of Their Own": *JazzTimes*, March 1999

"Musicians in Need": *JazzTimes*, July/August 2002

"When Dizzy Liberated Himself": *JazzTimes*, April 1999

"Testosterone Is Not a Musical Instrument": *Jazz-Times*, June 2001

The Rainbow of Country Music

"Blues Brothers Under the Skin": *Wall Street Journal*, May 1, 1998

Willie Nelson: "Honk Tonk Gypsy": *Wall Street Journal*, August 25, 2000

"Those Cheatin' Hearts": *Wall Street Journal*, September 4, 1998

Delbert McClinton: "Lone Star Troubadour": *Wall Street Journal*, September 28, 2001

Dale Watson: "Hard Country, Soft Heart": *Wall Street Journal*, January 4, 2002

"From 1970s Longhair Rockers to Bluegrass Icons": *Wall Street Journal*, August 8, 2002

Don Rigsby: "The Sound of His Kentucky Heritage": *Wall Street Journal*, November 12, 2003

The Farther Rainbow

"American Folk Songs, Direct from the Field": *Wall Street Journal*, November 20, 1997

"Folk Lives, Thanks to the Songcatchers": *Wall Street Journal*, June 7, 2001

"American Routes: Waters Roots of Folk": *Wall Street Journal*, February 10, 2000

"A Gift from America to the World": *Wall Street Journal*, April 16, 2002

Jazz Ahead

"End of Jazz: Hold That Note": *Wall Street Journal*, June 1, 2001

"Sonny LaRosa's Elementary School of Jazz": *JazzTimes*, December 2002

"Cutting Down Solos to Get to the Cutting Edge": *JazzTimes*, December 2000

"History Lessons Via Jazz": *Wall Street Journal*, January 5, 2001

Toshiko Akiyoshi: "Rising from the Abyss": *Wall Street Journal*, August 21, 2003

"The Newest Jazz Generation": *JazzTimes*, May 2003

"Categorizing the Future of Jazz": *JazzTimes*, April 2003

Last Chorus

"The Lion, Fats, and My Other Mentors": *Wall Street Journal*, December 30, 2003

INDEX